BROOKLAND

The Mature Student's Handbook

ACCES

D0317053

www.skills4study.com – the leading study skills website with FREE study tips, downloads and advice

Palgrave Study Skills

Authoring a PhD
Business Degree Success
Career Skills
Critical Thinking Skills
e-Learning Skills (2nd edn)
Effective Communication for
   Arts and Humanities Students
Effective Communication for
   Science and Technology
The Exam Skills Handbook
The Foundations of Research
The Good Supervisor
Great Ways to Learn Anatomy and
   Physiology
How to Manage your Arts, Humanities and
   Social Science Degree
How to Manage your Distance and
   Open Learning Course
How to Manage your Postgraduate Course
How to Manage your Science and
   Technology Degree
How to Study Foreign Languages
How to use your Reading in your Essays
How to Write Better Essays (2nd edn)
How to Write your Undergraduate
   Dissertation
The International Student Handbook
IT Skills for Successful Study
Making Sense of Statistics
The Mature Student's Guide to Writing (2nd edn)
The Mature Student's Handbook
The Palgrave Student Planner
The Personal Tutor's Handbook

The Postgraduate Research Handbook
Presentation Skills for Students
The Principles of Writing in Psychology
Professional Writing (2nd edn)
Researching Online
Research Using IT
Skills for Success
The Study Abroad Handbook
The Student's Guide to Writing (2nd edn)
The Student Life Handbook
The Study Skills Handbook (3rd edn)
Study Skills for Speakers of English as
   a Second Language
Studying Arts and Humanities
Studying the Built Environment
Studying Business at MBA and Masters Level
Studying Economics
Studying History (3rd edn)
Studying Law (2nd edn)
Studying Mathematics and its Applications
Studying Modern Drama (2nd edn)
Studying Physics
Studying Programming
Studying Psychology (2nd edn)
Teaching Study Skills and Supporting
   Learning
The Undergraduate Research Handbook
Work Placements – a Survival Guide for
   Students
Writing for Nursing and Midwifery Students
Write It Right
Writing for Engineers (3rd edn)

Palgrave Study Skills Literature

General Editors:John Peck and Martin Coyle

How to Begin Studying English Literature
   (3rd edn)
How to Study a Jane Austen Novel
   (2nd edn)
How to Study a Charles Dickens Novel
How to Study Chaucer (2nd edn)
How to Study an E.M.Forster Novel
How to Study James Joyce
How to Study Linguistics (2nd edn)

How to Study Modern Poetry
How to Study a Novel (2nd edn)
How to Study a Poet
How to Study a Renaissance Play
How to Study Romantic Poetry (2nd edn)
How to Study a Shakespeare Play (2nd edn)
How to Study Television
Practical Criticism

The Mature Student's Handbook

Lucinda Becker

palgrave
macmillan

© Lucinda Becker 2009

All rights reserved. No reproduction, copy or transmission of this
publication may be made without written permission.

No portion of this publication may be reproduced, copied or transmitted
save with written permission or in accordance with the provisions of the
Copyright, Designs and Patents Act 1988, or under the terms of any licence
permitting limited copying issued by the Copyright Licensing Agency,
Saffron House, 6-10 Kirby Street, London EC1N 8TS.

Any person who does any unauthorized act in relation to this publication
may be liable to criminal prosecution and civil claims for damages.

The author(s) has/have asserted his/her/their right(s) to be identified
as the author(s) of this work in accordance with the Copyright, Designs
and Patents Act 1988.

First published 2009 by
PALGRAVE MACMILLAN

Palgrave Macmillan in the UK is an imprint of Macmillan Publishers Limited,
registered in England, company number 785998, of Houndmills, Basingstoke,
Hampshire RG21 6XS.

Palgrave Macmillan in the US is a division of St Martin's Press LLC,
175 Fifth Avenue, New York, NY 10010.

Palgrave Macmillan is the global academic imprint of the above companies
and has companies and representatives throughout the world.

Palgrave® and Macmillan® are registered trademarks in the United States,
the United Kingdom, Europe and other countries.

ISBN-13: 978-0-230-21026-4
ISBN-10: 0-230-21026-0

This book is printed on paper suitable for recycling and made from fully
managed and sustained forest sources. Logging, pulping and manufacturing
processes are expected to conform to the environmental regulations of the
country of origin.

A catalogue record for this book is available from the British Library.

10 9 8 7 6 5 4 3 2 1
18 17 16 15 14 13 12 11 10 09

Printed and bound in China

Contents

Introduction

As a reader of this book you are probably either already a mature student or will soon be entering a course of study as a mature student. This means, of course, that you are already successful in several ways. You have successfully reached a point in your life where you are able to become a mature student, you have succeeded in finding a course of study that suits your needs, and, in buying this book, you have shown your determination to capitalise on this position and succeed as a mature student.

Statistically, you are already in an enviable position: mature students tend to excel in their chosen courses, and there are many reasons for this. They are generally more focused than their younger counterparts and can use their life experience within their study. If all of this seems a bit too good to be true, it is also worth bearing in mind that some mature students struggle with some aspects of studying, and even if they succeed in the end, this struggle can make the journey far harder than it needs to be – and that is why this book has been written. It is designed to help you to identify your strengths as a student (and there will be plenty of these, even if they do not all spring to your mind immediately) and to make best use of them. If you have weaknesses (and all students do, in one way or another) then these too will be explored and practical suggestions made as to how you can overcome or eradicate them.

Of course, there is no 'typical' mature student: you might be in your early twenties or have recently retired; you perhaps have a young family or you may be living alone; you might be dovetailing paid work and online or part-time study or be a full-time student. Your situation in life is as unique as you are, but you will have some things in common with other mature students, however different their lives seem at first glance.

● Why this book?

At this point you might be wondering why this particular book is the best guide for you. If all students have some weakness, why do you need a guide specifically aimed at mature students? Beyond the practical aspects of such a guide – the examples in this book, for example, will more nearly fit your circumstances than those in a guide for less experienced students – it is also important for you to focus on your needs and strengths in a way that makes more sense to mature students. Younger students, fresh out of school or college, for example, are unlikely to need much help with understanding the principles of coursework, as they will have lived and breathed coursework for several years already. A mature student might be far less familiar with this aspect of education. What a younger student is likely to need, though, is a lot of help with basic time management, whereas a mature student's life experience usually make issue. This book does give guidance on time management, but in a way tha_ most sense to those students who are already used to juggling life.

● Why this author?

I was myself a mature student when I first began to study. From A levels, through professional training courses, to a degree and finally a doctorate, I managed the demands of a working life, studying and a family. And I did it badly – for some of the time. Over the last ten years I have taught undergraduates of all ages and have devised and delivered professional development courses, including distance and e-learning courses; I have found out during that time that I was not alone in this. I wasted a lot of my time reinventing the wheel, trying to do things in new 'student' ways that I could perfectly happily – and far more easily – have done in my old ways. I worried about the wrong things, at the wrong times, and generally made life hard for myself; and I have seen countless mature students do exactly the same thing over the years.

So, that is what this guide is all about: helping you to avoid the pitfalls, encouraging you to use your talents, and guiding you through your course of study in the most effective way, to make it an enjoyable, and far more successful, experience.

● You are not alone . . .

Even on a course with a relatively high number of mature students, it is all too easy to feel alone, as if you are the only student to be facing your particular problems, or to be negotiating your particular hurdles. Although you try to convince yourself that others must be struggling in similar ways, it can be difficult to share your concerns with them, especially if you are studying on a course where you are outnumbered by younger students. As your course progresses you will find that the gap between mature and younger students is far less wide than you might have supposed. One of the joys of studying is discovering how shared interests break down barriers between people, but this may not be enough to help you when you are staring at a problem and feel unable to solve it alone.

The sense of isolation that this feeling brings with it is damaging, not only to you as a person, but also to the progress of your studying, but the sections in this book will show you that the challenges you face are quite usual in your circumstances. By seeing that you are not alone, I hope you will gain a stronger sense of yourself, your goals and your talents.

Feeling part of a mature students' community, which is spread throughout all areas of study and around the world, is a crucial step in achieving success. Drawing on the experience of others, and using the techniques that they have found effective, you will save yourself time and trouble, which will leave you more space in life to enjoy your success.

● How this book can help

You will probably use this book in several ways. You might be in a position, right now, to read the guide from cover to cover, which I hope you would find enjoyable. It is more likely that you will dip into it over the coming weeks and months. Whichever way you use it, I hope it is a book you will return to again and again as your course progresses.

With this in mind, the guide has been designed to offer you advice in several different ways. The text is deliberately broken up into manageable chunks of information: these chunks of information are intended to be used in various ways. The guide is divided into sections which can be used to give you an overview of an area or as a practical source of support. There are checklists to tick, tables to complete, charts to fill out – in short, this is a *doing* book as much as it is a reading book. It will also become a completely personalised book, too, allowing you to look back on the notes you made and the responses you gave earlier in your course, showing you how far you have come. The checklists may also be downloaded free from the following website, which will allow you to have as many copies as you like: www.skills4study.com.

If you feel confident in one area, you might just read the overview of that section so as to confirm what you know already. In other areas you will spend longer working through the exercises, but never too long: none of the exercises are too time consuming, so they will not take you from your studies for long. You are likely to read some sections in planning for a specific event, such as a presentation or an exam. In this case, you will find the checklists particularly useful, especially when you are at the stage of last-minute preparations.

Other areas will be useful to you as aids in the general development of your proficiency as a student. The step-by-step guides are designed to take you as easily as possible through key aspects of study skills, without the need to wade through yards of jargon or irrelevant theory; highlighted words will alert you to the key point of a section. After the general overview in each section, the exercises are designed to help you put the theory into practice. After most of the exercises there is a more detailed explanation, which you will only need as a support to that exercise.

Sometimes, of course, we all get stuck, knowing that we need some help but finding it difficult to work out just what guidance we need. This problem is particularly acute for mature students, who might be unfamiliar with some of the learning situations they face. For this reason, there is a list of suggestions at the end of each section as to where you might go next in order to keep developing your skills.

● Whichever type of learner you are . . .

You might be any type of student – you could be involved in an e-learning course, you could be a part- or full-time student, you could be undertaking a distance learning course or be staggering your learning over many months or years. Luckily, this book will be relevant to you whichever form your study takes. The exercises are drawn from many methods of study, and there is a good reason for this. Although you might feel very different from a student who is studying on a course that is structured differently from your own, the fundamental skills you will both need for success will be similar – in many cases, they will be identical. There are plenty of academic-sounding names for these skills, but in essence they are related to your everyday experience as a student; they are the fundamental building blocks of your success, and that is what this guide is all about.

1 Seminars, Study Workshops and Tutorials

Courses outside the school syllabus tend to be taught in two ways: through lectures, which can be given to a large number of students at a time, and usually do not involve any interaction between teacher and students, and through small group learning. These latter sessions can be called a variety of names (seminars, study workshops or tutorials) and this can be a bit confusing. **Tutorials** sometimes refer to a group learning situation, but might equally refer to a one-to-one session with an academic who is giving feedback on an assessed piece of work.

For clarity, **seminars** here are taken to be small learning groups, gathering regularly throughout a course either to talk through the issues raised in lectures or to work more generally on a module. Some courses are taught entirely by seminars, with no lectures. On your course they may be called **study workshops** (or **discussion groups**, or **learning sessions**, or **classes**) but the principal activity will be the same: a group of up to 16 or so students, working under the leadership of an academic on a specific topic, in sessions which usually last for one to two hours. Some seminars are fairly loosely organised: you may just have to turn up, usually having done some reading in advance, and talk through your ideas. Others may be far more rigidly structured, perhaps with student presentations or specific analytical tasks to carry out as a result of your preparatory reading and research.

Most academics love having mature students in their seminar groups, for the simple reason that they will actually talk! Students coming into further study straight from school or college develop the uncanny ability to remain silent, however much they are prompted, for as long as is needed until they can escape from the room. Mature students usually feel socially obliged to say something just to break that silence – much to the relief of the seminar leader. I remember cringing through agonising seconds of silence, desperately hoping that someone else would speak, knowing that I would, inevitably, break any silence that went on longer than 20 seconds. This led to seminars being a form of slow social torture, as I teetered between the unpleasant tension of silence and the problem of thinking up something intelligent to say. Of course, it did not take long for the other students in my seminar group to work this out, learning quickly that their silence would lead to my speaking.

The problem with this response is that a seminar can then become a one-to-one conversation between tutor and mature student and, once this is established, it is difficult to break the pattern. It is up to you to hang back occasionally, aware that the tutor knows that you will be ready to answer the question or lead the discussion if he or she catches your eye, but giving a chance to the less talkative students who might simply have been silent in the early sessions from shyness.

The list below will help you to prepare as you approach a series of seminars:

- When you get the seminar timetable, if the time is not possible for you, speak to whoever organises the timetable to try to change groups before the seminar series begins.
- If this is not possible, try to get to the first seminar and ask the tutor if it is possible to change the seminar time.
- Some tutors give out details of each seminar in advance, so check the notice-board and your emails regularly in the week before the first seminar.
- Read through the materials in advance, but also make notes so that you have an outline of the material in your mind before you begin to discuss it in a seminar.
- If you aren't clear about something you have read, a seminar is the perfect place to raise this, so note your questions in advance.
- Seminars are not just for focusing on one topic – your seminar tutor will be able to help with practical details of the course (assignment deadlines and so on) so prepare these queries too.
- Every seminar will not be of equal value to you. If you know you are going to examine a particular topic in an assignment, do a draft plan of the assignment before the seminar, so that you can ask the questions which will be of most use to you in your task.
- If the seminar series involves student presentations, decide in advance whether you would prefer to do a single or group presentation, and which week of term would suit you best to give your presentation, or which topic in the series you would prefer to cover. Students usually do not think this through before the first seminar, and then just put their names down for any available slot, rather than the best one for them.

● Seminar presentations

Not all seminar series include student presentations, but if presentations are used, they tend to take one of three forms:

- A **brief introduction** to a topic by a student, usually of ten minutes or so, followed by a group discussion led by the seminar tutor.
- A more **substantial presentation**, of perhaps 20 to 30 minutes, during which the student (or students) will give an overview of the topic, and also go on to outline critical debate surrounding the subject, perhaps including specific critical questions which are then discussed by the group, led by the seminar tutor.

- A fully **student-led seminar**, which would include a prese
  by discussion led by the student (or students) who gave th'

Each of these formats presents a different challenge, and the chapter on presentations in this guide will help you with the detail of how to give a successful presentation, but the points below will guide you through much of the process:

- Always confirm in advance which type of seminar you are giving – it is difficult if you are caught out, thinking that you are just giving a brief presentation and then finding that you also have to lead an hour's discussion.
- If you are to present in a group (usually two or three students) make sure that you divide the presentation tasks before you begin to prepare. You will probably each take one aspect of the topic, and decide at the outset how much time each speaker will be allocated and, if necessary, whether just one of the presenters is going to lead the discussion, or whether you are all going to be involved in that part of the seminar. This is important because some students prefer not to give a presentation, but are happy to lead a discussion or answer questions: you need to play to your strengths as a group.
- Although seminars are not very formal occasions, you will still need to stick to the time that has been allowed for your presentation, and you will need to check in advance whether you are expected to prepare handouts, and whether you will be able to use a data projector, or an overhead projector.
- Make sure that you know whether you are being assessed on your performance or not. Although you will want to give a good presentation regardless, if you are being assessed you might be handing in your notes and handouts at the end of the presentation, so you will have to prepare them with this in mind.
- Assume that the students in the seminar group who are listening to the presentation will have done very little preparation: they are probably prioritising their tasks by working on their own presentations. You will need to make sure that you give a brief, and very basic, overview of the topic before you begin on the more detailed issues you want to cover.

Tutorials

It can be daunting, facing a one-to-one session with a tutor to discuss your recent assignment or presentation or to talk through your dissertation or project plan (especially if you are disappointed with your assignment mark or have no idea yet about your dissertation). This is especially true if you do not have previous, or recent, experience of tutorials, or if you do not know the tutor very well.

The temptation in this situation (a temptation to which many students succumb regularly) is simply to see it as an unavoidable ordeal, during which you will try to smile a

.ot, say very little, and escape as soon as possible. This works quite well as a survival plan, but is far less effective if you actually want to gain anything out of the tutorial. Checklist 1 will help you to make it a much more positive experience.

CHECKLIST 1

	✔
Find out in advance whether it is a one-to-one session or if there are to be two or three of you involved. Don't be put off if it is a one-to-one session – this will give you a better chance to get more help.	
Ask around to see if you are likely to have to read your essay or plan aloud or not – this can be a bit of a challenge if you are not prepared for it.	
If you are receiving feedback on an essay or other written assignment, try to ignore the mark you got when you are preparing for the session. A very good or a disappointing mark can put you off asking what you really need to know.	
Read through the work before the tutorial and prepare a series of questions. You can expect your tutor to lead some of the discussion, but it is far more useful to you if you have some questions ready, especially if you are nervous.	
Compare this piece of work with other assignments that have been marked to see if you can see any patterns emerging. A tutorial is the best place to get help with any study skills problems you have (planning, grammar, formal writing and so on), but remember that the tutor will not have seen every piece of work that you have produced, and so will need some help from you in spotting these patterns.	
If you are intending to develop the topic of study under discussion, perhaps to do a further course in this area or to do an extended project or dissertation in the same field, make this clear at the outset so that the tutor can advise you on how best to move forward and develop your ideas.	
If it is a planning tutorial, ideally you will want to be ready with the most detailed plan you can make, but be willing to change your mind. Email your plan in advance so the tutor can prepare too.	
Don't be afraid to take notes during the tutorial – it is so easy to forget most of what was said as soon as you leave the room. Be brave about asking questions if anything at all is unclear to you.	
After the tutorial, work through the notes you have made: email the tutor for further help if anything is unclear.	

© Lucinda Becker (2009), *The Mature Student's Handbook*, Palgrave Macmillan Ltd

Seminars, tutorials, workshops and study groups, unlike lectures, rely on good leadership and plenty of student involvement. The reward you gain for your efforts is not just the satisfaction of being involved, but the realisation that you are developing as a student, trying out new ideas and being guided towards your future research and study.

How to progress:

- ☐ Take as many opportunities as you can to speak up in a group situation, both within your course and outside.

- ☐ Presentations are always best practised to an audience, so enlist the help of family and friends as audience, and encourage them to ask questions to help guide you; often non-experts in a field will ask the questions that show up the obvious points which you have missed.

- ☐ If you find seminars daunting, take any opportunity to talk to your tutor in a one-to-one situation, so that you feel more comfortable with that tutor in a group situation.

- ☐ Student-led workshops are a good way to begin making your voice heard: this then makes it easier to speak up in seminars.

2 Attending Lectures

Lectures are the cornerstone of most courses of study, so you can expect to attend plenty of them. Although you will also use other resources to prepare your assignments, the lecture is often the basis of your first thoughts on a subject. Even if you are a distance learner, reading most of your lectures on the internet or from a study pack, you are likely to attend occasional summer schools or study weekends, and lectures will form part of these.

From the very beginning of my life as a mature student I enjoyed the sense of occasion that comes with a lecture; I loved being able to sit for an hour whilst someone talked to me about a subject, knowing that I had a vested interest in what was being said. Indeed, I now sometimes attend undergraduate lectures just for the pleasure of being entertained for an hour with no responsibility for having to do anything with the information I receive ... and that is the problem with lectures. It is difficult, when you first come to them, to work out quite what to do with all of that information. I remember starting off by thinking that I had to try to record every word. Writer's cramp soon banished that thought. Then I thought I should just listen, and record what seemed most important after the event. I abandoned that approach after just one lecture, as my anxiety levels reached fever pitch. So, I had to decide on a system which made it possible for me to feel confident that I had the information I needed, but that did not mean I had exhaustive and unstructured notes. I had to learn to become selective and efficient.

To make the most of lectures, it is worth thinking about the purpose of a lecture and your role within that. Lecturers generally try to achieve four things in a lecture:

1   Give you a **good grounding** in a subject area: this is why lectures are so useful; they save you hours of time in the library.
2   Offer you a sense of the **critical debate** around the subject: this stops you making a fool of yourself by barking up the wrong tree.
3   Share their **specialised knowledge** in one aspect of the subject: this will give you plenty of detail, but will only really be relevant to you if you are intending to study the subject area in more depth, perhaps to write an essay on it.
4   Provide you with a springboard for **further study**: this is the bit you need to capture; the guidelines offered in a lecture will help you to manage your study time.

Once you have looked at this list the challenge becomes clear: this is a great deal to take in during just one lecture. I will assume here that your lectures will each last an hour, and that is long enough for most students.

The pleasure of a lecture is that it is a 'live' experience: you are listening to an expert in the field and valuable information is being hurled at you at a great rate. And that can cause problems: how are you supposed to take in what is most useful to you? Some students find that lectures make them anxious, and they spend their whole time worrying about missing a single word or thought; others find them a disappointment because they never seem to use their lecture notes after the event.

There are two apparent solutions to these problems, which students sometimes try out. The first is only to attend those lectures which you know will be really useful to you. The second is to try to take down the lecture in its entirety, either by recording it or using a laptop to capture each word. Neither of these approaches works. You won't know which are the most relevant lectures until you have been to them, and recording lectures, or typing them in full as they are given, is a colossal waste of your time. You will come out of the lecture having done very little analysis of the material. For an hour's lecture, you will then spend two hours after the event working through the recording, or your verbatim notes, trying to put them into some sort of order. Except, of course, you might not, because by then the next lecture will be due, so you run the real risk of approaching your exams with a pile of guilt-making lecture tapes or laptop files which you never quite got around to assessing. Unless you have good reason to do so, avoid taking this approach.

● Preparing for lectures

By far the best way of making lectures work for you is to understand your role in the process and to prepare for each lecture with this in mind.

Before each lecture, there are four things to do to prepare:

1   Make sure that you have the **lecturer's contact details**: often a lecturer will give just one lecture on a course, and you need to know how to get more information should you need it.

2   Read the **details of the lecture** carefully: often students are given the synopsis of a lecture in advance, which will help you to decide which sections of the lecture will be of most value to you.

3   Do any **advance reading** you have been asked to do, so that you have a grounding in the subject area. (Although, if you don't get the chance to do this, still attend the lecture!)

4   Decide how the lecture will fit into your **overall study needs**. Perhaps it will be relevant to a presentation you are giving, or it is aimed towards some assessed work you have to do, or it is a general background lecture.

This last is perhaps the most important point: if it is a general lecture, you will probably come out with writer's cramp, having tried to write most of the points down. If, on the other hand, it is a lecture that you know will come in handy for an essay or presentation, you might be focusing far more closely on some sections rather than others.

Making lecture notes

Now comes the art of making lecture notes. In a lecture you need to do three things, as shown in Figure 1.

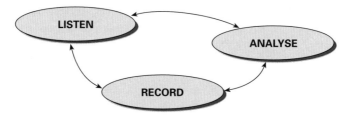

Figure 1

At some points you will just be listening, working out where the lecture is going next; at other times you be analysing what you have just heard; you will also be trying to record what you need in the most succinct and useful way. In fact, for most of the lecture you will be doing all three of these things simultaneously. That is why there is an art to making lecture notes: you have to juggle all of these balls in the air and come out with workable notes.

In the first box below there is an extract from a lecture (this extract happens to be for a Film Narrative course, and would take about ten minutes in a lecture theatre) and in the second box is an example of what the lecture notes might look like for this lecture. As you read through the first box, you might like to make your own notes on the lecture, so that you can compare these with the example notes I have given.

> One of the things you might have asked yourself is why this course is called 'Film Narrative'. Why not 'Film Studies'? Or 'Great Films You Should Watch'? Actually it is neither of these things. It is not a film studies course in the traditional sense, and none of the lecturers on the course would argue that every single film on the course is 'great'. But, every film on the course is important to our purpose, which is exploring film narrative.
>
> Throughout this lecture I will be referring to films and novels, filmmakers and novelists, and your handout gives you the details of these texts and their creators, just in case you are not familiar with them yet.
>
> The reason why we have chosen to devise and deliver a course which explores film from a narrative point of view rests, to some extent, with us as a department. We deal with literature, and literature is based upon narrative, so film narrative is a logical extension of this interest. Every piece of writing, and most pieces of speech, have a narrative.➡

From the humblest text message to the most complex novel, we can discern, if not always in a very conscious way, the presence of narrative. In fact, text messaging is really interesting for the huge leaps in narrative structure it is creating as a result of the limitations of space – James Joyce and Virginia Woolf would be proud of you all!

Anyway, to get back to the point: every piece of writing creates narrative, both real and imagined, implicit and explicit, and that is what we are interested in on this course. Narratives inevitably raise expectations, and this is a crucial part of storytelling: knowing what the audience expects and then either fulfilling or undermining those expectations.

First, it might be a good idea to dispel any confusion you might have about certain terms. Narrative can be used to describe speech, which is included in some, but not all, of our films on the course. Speech is, of course, an important part of a narrative. In the oral narrative tradition it is the only part of the narrative. But on this course it is of interest only in as much as it supports our main themes, and it is always interesting to note how few direct quotes from films are given in film criticism, as opposed to literary criticism.

The word 'narrator' also shares a root with narrative, and you will be considering the role of the narrator, in both films and writing, during your studies, but again this is not the principal focus of our course.

So let's focus on the course title: Film Narrative. The word 'narration' derives from the Latin *narrare*, 'to give an account of'. *Narrare* in turn derives from *gnarus*, meaning 'knowing' and is hence related to the English 'ignore', 'recognise' and, distantly, 'to know'. What is interesting about this word is the way it developed. Most usually we would expect a noun, in this case 'narration', to be a development of a verb, in this case 'to narrate'. However, with narration the development is back to front. 'Narration', the noun, came first, with 'to narrate' arriving considerably later. Indeed, in the eighteenth century the verb 'to narrate' was heavily criticised for being inelegant.

What might this history of the word be telling us about how our society has viewed narrative? We clearly viewed the narrative as more important than the narrator for many years, and this is in keeping with the oral tradition of storytelling, where the story was all. A different storyteller might tweak things a bit (this is not much different from traditional pantomimes, which in many ways carry on this tradition) but essentially the story was the star. This will be an interesting point for you to consider as this course progresses. In what ways, and to what extent, is the narrative the predominant element in the films you are studying? And to what extent do other elements – the impact of the director, or the star system, or the inexorable rise in new technology – detract from this predominance? Or maybe they simply support it? We have chosen the films, of course, because they all share a strong sense of narrative, and because they do interesting things with narrative, but there will still be competing demands on your attention from other aspects of film-making, and this will tell you something about how film narrative works.

A good place to start exploring film narrative is to look at narrative forms with which you are already familiar. I am thinking here of the novel form in particular. Early novels were usually structured on the basis of a chronological narrative, with the author describing events and the feelings of the characters, often with an omniscient narrator helping the reader to understand what was happening. In some ways the narrator was not dissimilar from the chorus in a Greek tragedy, telling the audience what to think and trying to sway its moral response to the drama which was unfolding on stage. If we think of an early novel such as *Tom Jones* we can see the importance of the narrator. This did not, of course, mean that early novelists could not dispense with a 'third person' narrator – *Gulliver's Travels* and *Pamela* are good examples of an attempt by the novelist to immerse the reader in a first-person narration.

To produce a chronological narrative did not, of course, satisfy novelists for long,   ➜

and soon traditional narratives with omniscient narrators were read and enjoyed along-side more daring and complex narratives. So, for example, we might remember Charlotte Bronte's *Jane Eyre*, with its famous last line, delivered by the narrator: 'Reader, I married him', alongside her sister's *Wuthering Heights*, in which we appear to be offered a straightforward, narrator-led story, only to find the novelist taking us in twists and turns through a complex narrative, with at least two framing devices and a chronological sweep which can, at times, be difficult to follow, if not intellectually then at least emotion-ally.

Film has never followed quite this pattern. It has at the very least nodded at the possi-bility of huge sweeps of time right from the outset, although, as with novels, truly complex narratives on screen (rather than by implication) took some time to develop. Thus in *Broken Blossoms* we see a chronological narrative, but we are taken through vast swathes of time and across two continents in just moments on screen. Imagine how long this would take to depict in a novel. This is one of the huge advantages of film – the ability to move easily and speedily through time and space. However, this ability did not always free the filmmakers from a novel-like format. For an audience more used to novels or short stories than film, a film such as *The Big Sleep* still offered its original audi-ence what seem a little like chapter headings between scenes, and this device can still be seen in the most recent film on the course – *The Football Factory* makes clear distinctions between its chapter-like scenes.

Even with the ability to twist narratives, novelists inevitably pushed the boundaries further. The development of 'stream of consciousness' writing, with its focus on interior monologue, took the novel to new places. No longer were we external observers of action – now the reader had the chance to enter the minds of the characters, to begin to under-stand their motivation and emotions in a way never before attempted. The problem with this for some novelists, although not all, was that the exploration of the human mind in print necessarily reduced the geographic and narrative scope of the novel. If you are to enter the intimate thoughts of a character, it seems that something must be sacrificed. Take, for example, Virginia Woolf's *Mrs Dalloway*. It is a fascinating and persuasive account of one woman's day, but it is no more than a day – there is simply no space to make the external narrative more complex or any longer than that.

Herein lies the problem for novelists. They may fight against it all they like (and James Joyce fought pretty hard) but they are restricted by space, by the amount that can physi-cally be portrayed in a novel. This is one of the key differences between a novel and a film. Imagine that a novelist were to try to describe a child's feeling of horror as her monstrous father bore down upon her, intending to beat her senseless. She is perhaps thinking back to her mother, who might also have endured such treatment; maybe she is also wondering whether her mother fled the abuse or whether she was killed by this man. She is also puzzling out how she could have placated her father, knowing that she might have escaped this life of terror for another life, in which she would be cherished and protected by a Chinese man who clearly adores her. Even in this truncated and dispas-sionate description of events I have written nearly a paragraph – for a novelist trying to create the atmosphere, the emotion of the event, it would take maybe a page or so. For a filmmaker, in *Broken Blossoms*, all of this is condensed into a few seconds on screen, as we see a close-up of Lucy's face.

So, on this aspect of creating narrative, the filmmaker seems to win hands down. Except that there is a problem. If a filmmaker can enter the minds of his or her protago-nists, and show their feelings and motivation to the audience, there is a danger that what we see on screen is simply one person's version of events, that in fact film narrative is restrictive, with the director imposing a version of events on the audience, rather than ➜

allowing us to think and feel for ourselves. This problem is made most clear, perhaps, when films are made of classic novels. We make an emotional investment in novels, and part of that investment is to imagine that we know the characters and how they would respond to an event. When we watch, for example, a film version of a novel by Dickens, Austen or Dostoyevsky, we are likely to temper our enjoyment with a sense of irritation, convinced at times that the director has simply got it wrong.

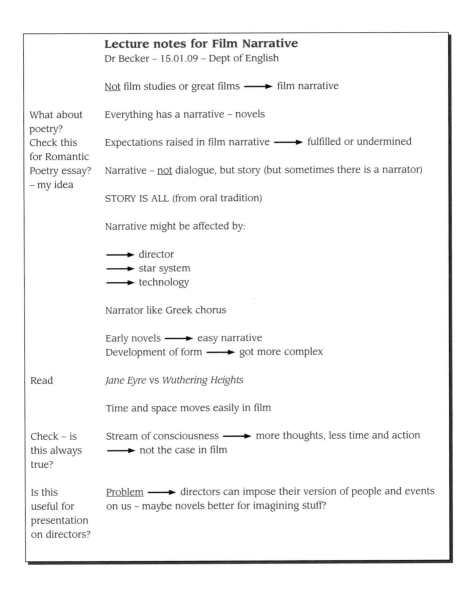

Lecture notes for Film Narrative
Dr Becker – 15.01.09 – Dept of English

<u>Not</u> film studies or great films ⟶ film narrative

What about poetry?   Everything has a narrative – novels
Check this for Romantic Poetry essay? – my idea   Expectations raised in film narrative ⟶ fulfilled or undermined

Narrative – <u>not</u> dialogue, but story (but sometimes there is a narrator)

STORY IS ALL (from oral tradition)

Narrative might be affected by:

⟶ director
⟶ star system
⟶ technology

Narrator like Greek chorus

Early novels ⟶ easy narrative
Development of form ⟶ got more complex

Read   *Jane Eyre* vs *Wuthering Heights*

Time and space moves easily in film

Check – is this always true?   Stream of consciousness ⟶ more thoughts, less time and action
⟶ not the case in film

Is this useful for presentation on directors?   <u>Problem</u> ⟶ directors can impose their version of people and events on us – maybe novels better for imagining stuff?

● After the lecture

As you can see, these notes miss out whole sections of the lecture. For example, the student has decided that, however interesting it is, keeping a note of the development of the word 'narration' is not of any lasting value. The notes are made easier to take because the student has used abbreviations and arrows – you will find your own abbreviations with practice. Because the student is trying to listen and analyse, there is only time to record the key points of the lecture, but the student can be certain that the most important and relevant points (that is, the points which will be useful in the future) are all here.

One of the most important aspects of this record is the series of marginal notes, prompting the student to further research. The note 'my idea' here is vital – on looking back at these notes the student will know that this is a genuinely original idea, which can be pursued without worrying that it has been taken from anyone else.

Every now and then, when you have a bit of spare time (maybe once a week), set aside time to work through the lecture notes you have made and tidy them up. You might want to add a few points from the lecture that you still remember and now realise are more important than you first supposed. You might want to keep a **lecture notebook** to record some of the instructions to yourself (in this case, the plan to read *Jane Eyre* and *Wuthering Heights*). You will certainly want to transfer the points you highlighted as useful to essays or presentations onto separate pieces of paper, so that a whole series of these notes is ready for you when you start to plan – it makes the planning process so much easier.

To check how well you are developing your lecture note skills, you could use the tick boxes in Checklist 2 for your next few lectures. Once you are happy that you can tick all the boxes for these lectures, you can file each set of lecture notes away, confident that you are now ready to move on to the next challenge. Mastering lectures is also a milestone in your increasing sense of yourself as a student. They are, perhaps, an experience which is unique to students, so being able to walk into a lecture knowing that you are prepared and will gain maximum benefit from the experience is one of the things which marks you out as an established student. You will also find that your approach to other experiences in life changes subtly as a result: you begin to recognise and utilise more effectively many other learning opportunities in life, but you also become a more active listener, and this is an advantage in personal, professional and educational situations.

CHECKLIST 2

	Lecture title:	Lecture title:	Lecture title:	Lecture title:
Do I have the lecturer's contact details?				
Have I read a description or synopsis of the lecture in advance?				
Have I done the recommended reading for the lecture?				
Have I considered in advance how I expect this lecture to be useful?				
Did I get the right balance between listening, analysing and recording?				
Are my lecture notes brief enough?				
Have I checked them to see that I have enough detail?				
Have I transferred important information to a separate sheet, ready for an essay/presentation?				
Have I made a note to myself to do any extra reading from the lecture?				
Have I looked at 'my ideas' to see if they give me clues as to where to go next?				

© Lucinda Becker (2009), *The Mature Student's Handbook*, Palgrave Macmillan Ltd

How to progress:

☐ Practise making notes on TV or radio programmes, then read them back the following week to see how well the notes help you to recall what you saw or heard.

☐ Compare your lecture notes with those of fellow students.

☐ If you are given a lecture handout for future reference (rather than one to which you are expecting to refer during the lecture), avoid looking at the handout until you have made your lecture notes, and then compare how well your notes reflect the key points which the lecturer intended to make.

3 Reading Skills and Note Taking

Although there might occasionally be an area of your study where there are few books to read (if you are breaking new ground in a project, for example), in general there are just too many books to wade through on most courses. Or so it at first appears. There are two reasons for this: some students will have only very basic knowledge in their area of study, and so will need to read numerous guides to get them up to speed; and tutors are aware that many students will be needing supporting material at the same time, with the limited resources of any library, and so they make huge **reading lists** so that you have some chance of finding at least a few of the books still in the library when you need them.

However, neither of these points is obvious when you are first given a reading list for a course, and your first instinct might be to assume that every book on the list must be read – a daunting task. This is especially true for distance or part-time students whose courses may be spread over a longer period of time, so that they feel that they do, probably, have the time to read everything. When you add to the book list all of the other recommendations for internet sites, articles in journals and in-house material, it is easy to see why students can feel overwhelmed.

I assumed, without question, that I would have to read all of the texts on the first reading lists I was given as a student. When family and friends pointed out that 86 books seemed like a lot of reading for one term, I blithely told them that this must all be part of the student experience, and got reading … and reading … and reading. By the end of that term, blindness and madness creeping over me in equal measure, I was forced to admit my failure as a student: I simply could not keep up with the workload. In some desperation I went to see my personal tutor at the beginning of my second term and confessed my failure: I admitted that I had given up at the end of book number 79 and was not entirely sure that I was ready for student life.

At first I took my tutor's look of stupefaction to be a reflection of her horror at my ineptitude. She then patiently and (to my eternal gratitude) without even a snigger, explained to me that the reading list was no more than a guide to a range of texts available to me, given to students in the hope that they might read half a dozen of them. I felt stupid, but also hugely relieved. That night my children were well fed again, the washing was done and I actually watched television … and never again have I looked at any reading list as anything more than a polite suggestion as to reading I might like to undertake, if and when I have the need and the time.

If you look at it for a moment from a tutor's point of view you can see how huge reading lists happen: the tutor is concerned to give the best help possible to the students, and so in addition to lectures, seminars and practical sessions, the tutor scours the library or resource centre for every possible piece of useful material.

Faced with your reading lists, this is your chance to begin to exercise your critical judgement as a student and a scholar. There might be a time when you have a major project and a reading list of just ten items; in this case, you can happily look at them all, but never assume that you will have to read every item on every reading list; instead, work through the lists with a critical eye, bearing in mind the advice in this section.

● Types of texts

The first overview to take is to consider how you are taking in and using your knowledge – see Figure 2.

Once reading and note taking are seen in this light, they become active components of your course, rather than passive chores to be completed – and that allows you to take control. You first step in **achieving control** is to evaluate the pile of books that you currently have to hand. You can divide most piles of books into five sections:

- **Base texts**: these are the fundamental building blocks that you need for your course. You will usually buy them and refer to them time after time. In a course where you are familiar with the subject area you might own only one of these books; in a course where most of the material is new to you, you might need to buy several. These texts increase your confidence, making you feel more in control of your subject area.
- **Working texts**: these are vital – the lifeblood of your studying. They are often collections of essays, or journal articles, or internet pages. You are unlikely to read the whole book, journal or internet site, but you might return to each several times as your study needs change. There will be many of these texts in your life as you study, but you must have the confidence to read only those sections or essays which you really need: it is perfectly acceptable, indeed advisable, to take ten of these books out of the library and only read one chapter of each. These texts make you feel good: you will have a list of many of them, and they can be conquered relatively quickly.
- **Reference texts**: of course all of your texts are used for reference, but your relationship with these texts will be brief and productive. They are the books from which you just want the one perfect quote to support your argument, or the internet site where you want to look up one quick fact, or the journal article where you just want to look at the way some research findings have been laid out for the reader. For these texts, you might just skim through the index to see whether you need to go further, or read one short essay to confirm what you already think. These texts make you believe that you are making real progress in your work.

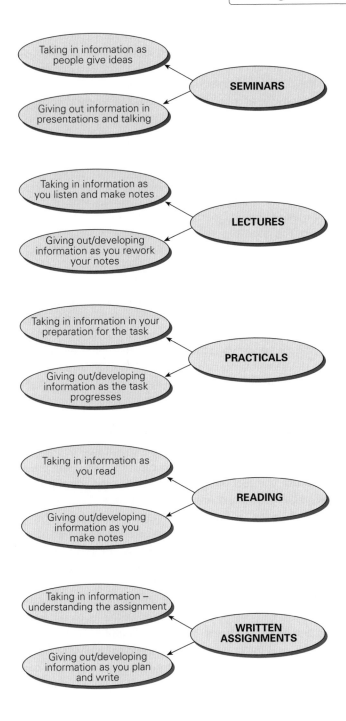

Figure 2

- **Useless texts**: these are the books or journals that lurk in the corner of the room. You feel you really should read them, and somebody told you they found them really useful, but every time you try, you just end up muddled or despondent. One of the major milestones in taking charge of your reading is when you come to accept that some books just aren't worth your trouble. Perhaps the writing style doesn't suit your taste, or the book is too basic or advanced for your needs at the moment, or (and this happens) it is just a badly written book. Never let books bully you: if you have a useless text, be ruthless; take it back to the library and firmly put it back on the shelf. It will still be there later if you suddenly need it again.

- **Easy-read texts**: these texts have nothing to do with your studying, but that does not make them unimportant. They are the gossip magazines you read on the train, or the latest bestseller that you read in bed at night. They are important not because of their content, but because of their purpose: they allow you to escape. It can be difficult to sleep at night if you have just been reading a textbook, and it is impossible to study for every waking moment of the day. Your brain needs time to relax, but that does not mean that you have stopped working. As you read the easy novel or article, your brain is gently, and subconsciously, assimilating the progress of the day. It is no surprise that we all have some of our greatest ideas in the shower after a good night's sleep, or at two in the morning after an evening off. These texts make you feel that you have a mental life beyond your studying: and they help with the studying too, so no feelings of guilt – perfect.

Now that you have these categories of text in your mind, it is time to carry out a '**text audit**'. The reason this is important is that an untargeted approach to reading is a time-wasting process. You will spend far too much of your precious study time reading books because you feel obliged to do so, or trawling through an entire book when only a few pages of the text are relevant to your needs, or take hours over an internet search which leads you down too many blind alleys. The specifics of your course will dictate how many texts you need of each type, but it is still possible to give a guide to how many would be expected for most types of course. If you were to look at the sum of the study texts that you have, the ideal ratio would be as shown in Table 1.

So, take a look at the texts you have with you right now, and identify each text as being in one of the five categories. Include journal articles (count each article as one, not each journal) and internet articles. Tally up the number of texts in each section and enter them in Table 2. You might have a similar ratio to that given above, in which case you know you are on course to have an effective reading time ahead of you. If your ratio is very different from the one above, you might want to think about why this is: are you keeping books too long, just in case you might need them again? Do you feel anxious about taking books back to the library even if they are useless to you? Do you struggle to see the relevance of texts? Do you make too many notes, and spend too much time

Type of text	Ratio
Base texts	1
Working texts	6
Reference texts	4
Useless texts	0
Easy-read texts	1

Table 1

Type of text	Ratio
Base texts	
Working texts	
Reference texts	
Useless texts	
Easy-read texts	

Table 2

reading single texts? Once you begin to answer these questions you will be able to work towards more productive reading methods.

● Tips for choosing books

Of course, you do not have to stick rigidly to reading lists, especially if your Students' Union or department runs a second-hand book stall. It can be productive to range more widely, but only if you stick to the rules of reading for study, and if you check the validity of the alternative texts you are using with your tutor. The rules are:

1   Check the date of publication: the vast majority of academic books become out of date as they are superseded by others. In some areas there will be classic texts that are still in use despite their age, but this needs to be confirmed.
2   Check the author: does your tutor rate this writer by, for example, including other works by the same writer on the reading lists?
3   Check the table of contents: you might only need to read one section of the text.
4   Check the index: is this writer referencing other writers on your reading lists? To agree or to disagree with them? Is this a good or a bad thing?
5   Read the first page, to make sure that the writing style is one you like: a dense or incomprehensible book must be firmly put on the 'useless texts' pile.
6   Check the structure: if you are tackling a new area you might need a single-authored text on the topic; if you are working up your ideas, a collection of essays is probably more useful; if you are about to write an essay, you might be looking at indexes for useful sections from which to quote.

Once you are happy about how to approach texts that are not on the reading lists, you can enjoy the benefits of **library serendipity**. Rather than just targeting the texts on your reading lists, take a few minutes to browse up and down the shelves of the relevant section of the library. As long as you apply the rules above, you are likely to find, and be able to use, some really useful books which nobody else on your course will have considered.

● Tips for choosing internet texts

Internet serendipity is more dangerous. If you find no useful books in your library browsing, you have probably wasted no more than a few minutes. If you are browsing the internet, you can easily waste hours of your time reading material that is interesting and engaging, but totally useless to you: articles which are out of date, or only peripherally relevant to your field, or factually inaccurate. It is easy to be tempted because the internet is so attractive, but follow these rules:

1   Check the **hard copy options**: if you find an article which seems relevant, you may find that the author has produced it elsewhere in a book or journal, and this allows you to work from a hard copy which you know has been proofread by the author and approved by a publisher.

2   Check for **peer review**: this is the process by which books and articles are judged by academics before they are published. Within this category on the internet would be web-based copies of professionally recognised articles. This is not to say that you must never use any other source on the internet, but you must be aware of its provenance.

3   **Handle the material appropriately**: if, for example, you find the papers from a conference you were unable to attend are published on the internet, you will want to look at them, but remember that these might not be the final word that the speaker has to say on a subject; it might reflect a work in progress.

4   Be aware of the **ephemeral nature** of the material: because internet sites can change frequently, make sure that you print out the pages that are vital to you, and note the full page address and the date on which you accessed any site.

5   Always, always **reference the material**: internet access might be 'free', but the material you glean is not 'free' for use without referencing. Because it is someone's intellectual property, you need to reference it just as meticulously as you would any published source.

6   Public sites are just that. Sites that are produced by non-experts, such as **internet encyclopaedia sites**, are fun to look at and they can give you a useful feel for an area, but you can never, ever guarantee that they will be reliable.

7   Keep cutting your search area: because the internet is such a vast source, the only way to approach it effectively is to have a **'study shopping list'** before you go online, and to stick rigidly to it, going only to sites which are of direct relevance, and cutting your search area as you go so that you stay focused.

8   Limit your time: it is amazing how fast a morning can go once you have logged on. Give yourself a **time limit**: this will help you to be ruthless about what you are prepared to spend time on and what you will discard.

9   **Check with your tutor**: if you are relying heavily on one particular site, or using the internet as your principal support for a piece of work, it is a good idea to send your tutor a list of the sites that you intend to use, just to make sure that they are respected and valid for your area of study.

● Tips on the honey bee method

If the traditional image of a student sitting for hours in a library taking notes does not appeal to you, you could consider another route favoured by mature students. This is to adopt the 'honey bee method' of assimilating information. It is a two-stage approach, which involves you collecting information (honey bee style) from your library or the internet, and then, at a later time, turning that information into useful material.

In gathering the material, it is a good idea to ask, before you even enter the library or turn on your computer, some limiting questions:

- How many books do I actually need? That is, how many books can I reasonably expect to work through before I am next back in the library or online?
- Do I need any books or internet sites to give me basic, background information?
- Do I need any books or internet sites to give me ideas on where to go next in my work?
- Do I need any books to help me to work out how to structure my approach to my next assignment?
- Should I take out just one book or view just one internet site which will give me a slightly different approach to the one I have been taking?
- Do I have specific titles of books or internet sites already?

Borrowing books is fairly straightforward – the internet can be more of a problem. I would urge you to print off the pages from the internet site that you feel will be useful to you. This prevents you from spending too long just browsing through sites, and it allows you to work on the material later on. Browsing the internet for study material should be like a well-organised shopping trip: you know in advance what you want, you go in and get it, and you leave – decisively.

Try placing a time limit on each library visit or internet session: the point of the honey bee approach is to speed up the information-gathering stage of the process so that you have more time for analysis and assimilation of the material. If you put yourself under moderate time pressure you are more likely to be ruthless about weeding out the material that is less useful to you.

To reduce the likelihood of losing time following a library visit, ask yourself one essential question: how much of this text do I need? For any area of study there are unlikely to be more than one or two books which you need to take home and read more or less in their entirety, but there will be many more that you can pick apart in the library. If you just need some quick references for a written assignment, you can use the index to find the relevant pages and then simply photocopy those pages: a book is suddenly reduced to six or eight photocopied pages.

Once you have the material, you are ready to move on to the next stage, and this requires some planning. It is best to set aside specific times for making notes on the texts you have borrowed (or the sections you have photocopied) and the internet pages you have printed. Little and often is the best rule of thumb here: because for the most part you will only have sections of books to work on, it is easy to set aside an hour at a time, rather than having to allow an entire day on note taking.

There is a danger here, of course: the temptation simply to file your copied sections of books or your printed internet pages will be strong, but this is always a disaster. You will be piling up work for yourself in the future, and you might find yourself gathering more and more material rather than fully exploiting what you have already: a manic honey bee, constantly circling the hive, is far less productive than one that is actually prepared to sit and make the honey, so here is how to do it:

1   Set yourself a **time limit** to work through a section of your material, and try to stick to it. If you spend a lot more time than you had planned in your first session, you are less likely to be motivated to return to the task because it will become too daunting. Remember that, whilst you might spend an hour or so working on the photocopied notes from one book, the next batch of material might take only a few minutes.

2   Be ready to use **two methods of recording**: have a pen and paper ready to make notes, but also have a highlighter pen beside you. In some cases you might just be highlighting a few relevant quotes for fairly immediate use, and will not need to waste time copying them out.

3   Before you even start to read, remind yourself of why you are reading this text. How will it help you? Is it for immediate use or for your long-term studying? Is it useful as a revision text? Is it helping you to understand the basics, or opening your mind to new possibilities?

4   Never make notes until you have read an **entire paragraph**. This is essential if you are to avoid simply copying out whole swathes of text. If the book or inter-net site is intended as a basic background to your area of interest, try to read an entire section or chapter before you make notes. There are two advantages to this technique: you are forcing yourself to make a judgement on how useful the material is before you make a note of it, which will help to develop your critical thinking, and you are having to remember the information before you write it down. Although you will still have the text in front of you to check the details, you will be amazed at how much information you will retain if you force your-self to remember the information for just a short while before you write it down in note form – especially useful if you have to take exams later in your course.

5   Always keep a **critical eye** on the usefulness of the book or internet site. If you are struggling to take in the information because of the way the text is written, or if you start to lose confidence in the material, put the text aside for a while and move on to the next one. When you return to the problematic text later you will be in a good position to decide whether the problem was yours (you had not grasped the subject area before you began to make notes on a detailed or in-depth study) or whether the text is perhaps less valuable than you had expected, and should be discarded or skimmed more briefly for any nuggets of useful information or good ideas.

6   At the end of each section or chapter, once you have made notes, consider your **overall position**. Do you need to read more of this text? Why? Should you move on to the next text? Why? By taking stock periodically you ensure that no time is lost, but also that you do not waste useful material – you will be moving on in a focused and motivated frame of mind.

7   Although it can feel counter-intuitive, **the breaks** you take during your note taking are often as important as the time you spend working. Regular breaks – even for just a few minutes whilst you take a quick walk or make a cup of tea – allow your mind to take an overview of your progress. It is during these brief breaks that you suddenly have a good idea, or find that several disparate ideas gel together, so try to take a short break every half an hour. Avoid doing anything that will lead your mind away from the work in hand, such as checking your emails or making phone calls. It is good to make a little distraction from the work, but not to become so distracted that you lose sight of where you are in your note making. Let your mind rest during the breaks and it will repay you.

8   Once you have highlighted or made notes on a text, take a few minutes to **produce a synopsis** of the material; this could save you hours later on when you are searching through your notes for the next project or for revision. To be able to glance through and see instantly what each text has to offer is hugely beneficial. The synopsis need only be brief, maybe in the form of a bullet-point list, or a paragraph outlining how you think this material fits into your overall studying, or a spider chart or mind map, if these suit you, for more complex material.

9   If you have a lot of material to cover, and your exams are not far away, it can be worth reducing your notes to brief points on **index cards**, for easier revision, but only do this if you can be sure that the cards will not be lying around for too long before you use them for revision, otherwise they could lose their impact.

10   Always copy down (or photocopy) the **complete reference** to any material which you have gathered and note the date on which you made the notes. Not only does this save you time later when you are preparing a bibliography, it also helps you to avoid the possibility of plagiarism.

CHECKLIST 3

	✔
Title of the books/journal articles/internet sites, for this session, with authors and editors:	
Full publication details (publisher's name, location and date of publication for each text) and pages covered in this session.	
Am I clear about why I am studying this text and how I will use the information I glean?	
What is my time limit for this session?	
Have I stuck to this limit?	
Did I plan in advance which texts needed full notes and which just needed highlighting?	
Did I stick to this plan?	

© Lucinda Becker (2009), *The Mature Student's Handbook*, Palgrave Macmillan Ltd

CHECKLIST 3 (continued)

	✔
Did I manage to read a section before making notes, for every text, every time?	
If not, what was the problem?	
Did I keep a critical eye on the usefulness of texts as I went along?	
Did I take stock at the end of every section or chapter on which I worked?	
Did I take breaks during this session, and were they the right sort of breaks (not too long or too short, without too many distracting activities during them)?	
Did I produce a synopsis of some sort for each text (bullet-point notes, or a brief paragraph, or a spider chart or mind map)?	
For revision material, did I produce revision cards for this material?	
Have I filed the complete set of material for each text in the right place?	

© Lucinda Becker (2009), *The Mature Student's Handbook*,
Palgrave Macmillan Ltd

Once you have completed your note making, you will get your reward, in the form of the pleasure you will take from placing the photocopy, your notes and your synopsis all in a plastic wallet and filing them away. Now, rather than having a pile of books, of uncertain value, you will have a series of folders which will be of immediate use to you when you need them.

● A reading notebook

Identifying useful texts need not be limited by the time you spend in the library or by your official reading lists. You will find that texts are mentioned all the time – in lectures, in seminars and classes, by your fellow students or guest speakers, even on radio or television programmes which touch upon your subject area. This can be a huge pressure on students – the sense that there is an ever-expanding list of titles out there, some of which may be mislaid or forgotten altogether as you are distracted by other tasks.

The most effective way to relieve this pressure is to create a reading notebook: an A5, hardback, lined notebook, in which you can jot down titles or authors who are mentioned to you in passing, or the most useful-looking texts from your reading lists, or texts recommended in lectures. Leave space after each initial note you have made so that you can fill in the full title and author's name, the location of the text in the library, and the full publication details. Also, leave a margin so that you can make a brief comment on the text. This is a pleasant way to spend the last half hour of a busy study day: browsing through the library or the online catalogues to fill in these details. Get in the habit of carrying your reading notebook around with you, so that you can capture texts in it whenever the chance arises.

Your reading notebook will help you to exercise your judgement over your potential reading. As you go through these texts, you can write comments such as 'no good' in the margin if a text is not going to be useful to you, or 'buy this' if you realise that it is an essential base text. The most satisfying margin note is the word 'done', to show that you have made notes and finished with the text. When you have a whole page of texts that have marginal notes, you will have the satisfaction of snipping off the corner of a page, to show that it is complete. This gives a feeling of control: you are on top of the task and have taken charge of your reading material.

A completed page of a reading notebook for a student studying nursing could look like the one in Table 3. I have included all the notes, which will have been made on several occasions.

As you will see, this chapter has been about wresting control from the morass of potential reading material available to you. Taking charge in this way will make you feel less stressed and will make your reading and note-making time far more productive. It will also allow some time for reflection. It is difficult to quantify the process of reflection: you cannot tick it off on a list of 'things to do', but it is essential if you are to change the

Done – good for presentation	*Palliative Care in the Community* By someone called Walters? George Walters and Elaine Rowe, Palgrave Macmillan, 2004, pp. 20–48
Done – OK for context essay?	Someone called Shouemakker wrote on Victorian nursing – in a journal somewhere? Relevant for context essay? Ingrid Shuemakker – 'Victorian Nursing and Its Relevance to Today', in *American Journal of Nursing*, 2001, Vol. III, Issue 36, pp. 20–29
No good	*The Theory and Practice of Nurse Prescribing in Hospitals in Sweden: A Case Study* Charlotte Bingley
Done	*Long Term Pain Management: A New Approach* Jack Chaucer – Nursing Publications, 2006, pp. 21–48
Done – good for dissertation	Conference paper by Dr Munroe on care for non-mobile patients? October Nursing Conference – check out online conference proceedings
No good	A book by Gillian Spenser on nurse dispensing in Hull? Out yet?

Table 3

way you look at your subject area and develop a better sense of how things work. If you do no more than take in masses of undigested information, you are in a poor position to use that information: it is in moments of reflection that you really develop as a thinker, so making the time to do this is vital, and that is the main point of taking control of your reading.

How to progress:

☐ This is a skill which always gets better with practice, so take the chance to summarise the information in anything you read. This might be a magazine article you have just read, or a pamphlet that came through your door. It is a fascinating process in itself, as you begin to grasp the main messages in everything you read, but it also creates the good habit of being able to summarise and prioritise information, quickly and accurately.

☐ Periodically, return to notes that you made earlier in the course – you should see some progress, with your notes being more concise, to the point and relevant to each task ahead of you.

☐ Spend a little time developing your own note-making code – symbols or words which will indicate to you that you need to research an area more, or that you agree with a point being made, or that you doubt the facts being presented. Use your codes consistently and make a key to decipher them – it is easy to forget what you meant when you look back at your notes in the future.

4 Planning

I love to plan: everything. From a simple shopping trip to a long-term work project, everything in my life is planned to perfection. This makes me very efficient; it also makes me, far too often, rigid in my thinking, too narrow in my approach and unwilling to see any possible way of tackling a problem but my own, perfectly planned way. At the beginning of my time as a mature student I had been out of education for over a decade, so I often found myself facing situations which I found daunting, and the way I responded to this was to stick to what I knew I could do: plan everything, instantly and sometimes with too little thought for the outcome. I refused to consider the option of different types of planning methods (my way was always the best way, as far as I could see) and I absolutely would not consider the possibility that plans could, and indeed should, be changed.

This approach served me surprisingly well as an undergraduate; it failed miserably once I moved on. Within three weeks of beginning my doctoral work I had planned my entire thesis – in minute detail – and I sat back and wondered what all the fuss was about. How could this thesis possibly take three years to complete? By the time I had written my thesis, I was writing from detailed plan number seven, and I decided upon my final title on the day I submitted. I had finally come to understand that planning is not just about organising information; it is about giving yourself some structured space within which to think. Coming to this realisation was both slow and painful. I wanted the comfort of beautifully arranged plans; I needed the challenge of changing my mind. Today I still plan everything in life, but I have come to accept that plans can change, that often they have to change if you are to get the best possible outcome, and the way to this acceptance for me was an increasing understanding of how plans could help me to think more clearly about what I had to say and what I wanted to achieve.

Although spider charts tend to be the most popular method of planning for students, and this is why they are used throughout this guide, there are other methods you might want to consider using. In this section, some of the most common planning methods are discussed, with an example of how they work in action.

A word of warning

For most students, planning becomes an everyday part of their studying life. They will find a method that suits them and use it for most of their output, varying the method only if the occasion calls for it. For just a few students, those who suffer from **organisa-**

tional dyslexia, planning can become a nightmare. You might not feel affected by the normal 'word blindness' we all associate with dyslexia – indeed, you might spell very well, and yet still find that the transition of ideas into words in a plan confuses you. If you regularly make plans and then ignore them, if you change your mind frequently about the best plan, if you endlessly cut and paste an essay because you just cannot work out the best way to structure your thoughts, you might suffer from organisational dyslexia. The good news is that your institution will be able to offer you effective help for this, but it makes sense to get a diagnosis and help as soon as you suspect that this might be the case for you.

● Are you a natural planner?

This is worth considering first. Even if you do not regularly plan everything you write or present, you might be a natural planner. If you make lists of what you have to do each week, if you go on holiday with a clear idea of what you will be doing, if you go food shopping with a list, and you fairly much stick to it, you are a natural planner. If none of these things apply to you, you are probably not a natural planner.

Either position can have its advantages. If you are a natural planner you will enjoy this chapter and you might develop these basic planning methods to suit your particular needs. Within a short time you will be using a selection of coloured pens to enliven your plans; they will become complex and you will feel confident about working from them. But beware: if you are a natural planner, you might discard all of these methods and simply make a list of headings and subheadings for each piece of work, and this is fine if it works for you, except that you might miss some information if you begin to plan too fast. You might also fall into the trap of making so many plans, of such detail, that you struggle to actually get around to the writing.

If you are not a natural planner, the novelty of thinking about planning will take you through this chapter. When you try out the plans in practice, you will probably stick to one planning method rigidly, because you know it works for you. You are still unlikely to plan everything, but you might enjoy the discipline of using one of these planning methods for some pieces of work – especially a large project such as a dissertation. The problem for you might be that, if you use a method that doesn't suit you, the planning process could make everything much less clear.

● Know the best planning method for each task

If you use a planning method that does not suit the way your mind works, you are almost better off not planning at all, as you will be confusing yourself by trying to map your ideas onto a system which is working against your normal thought processes. Try out the methods suggested here over the coming weeks and months, so that you can be confident that the method you are using is the best one for you.

Be ready to vary the method you use for different assignments. I have outlined below the type of assignment that lends itself to each planning method: you will not want to use a method which makes no clear sense to you, but you will probably find that different methods have varying value for differing situations. If you are working in a group situation, try to insist on a method which works for you – otherwise you might feel excluded from the planning process – but most of us can feel reasonably confident about using at least a couple of methods, so you will have options.

● Make a six-point plan before you get confused

Human beings find it surprisingly difficult to take in more than about **six main points** in anything we do – this is why the drop-down menus on most computer software packages usually give you between five and seven options before moving you on to the next set of options; it is also why we tend to use the same few settings on our washing machines, however complicated they are. Students often bemoan this idea, telling me that their area of study is so complicated that they simply cannot reduce what they have to say to six points, but many years of experience has taught me that, if you cannot reduce an essay, a presentation, even an entire dissertation, to six main points, you have got it wrong. Either you have not properly understood the assignment, and so are flailing around trying to cover all bases, or you are simply trying to tell your readers everything you know about the subject, without any clear idea of what they actually need to hear. This is perhaps the most painful thing about planning: deciding what to leave out, making a choice about which material is going to support your argument and which material is irrelevant and will do no more than blow your word count without achieving much.

The six-point plan acts as an intellectual insurance policy. You may well change your mind about your main points or, once you have considered the detail, each point might have 32 sub-points, but what it represents is your initial, gut reaction to the topic, and this is a valuable insight. Once made, you will put this six-point plan to one side. You will not slavishly follow all of the six points, but you will take the opportunity later to refer back to them again, to see how your thoughts have developed, and to make sure that you have not missed an entire section because you have become so engrossed in the detail.

For this chapter I am using as an example a project report. The student is studying business management, and has been asked to consider the merits of relocating an engineering company, Access Engineering, to a new site in a place called Easthaven. The initial six-point plan might look like this:

1   Details of the site and location.
2   Transport links.
3   Clients.
4   Advantages of the move.

5   Staff.

6   Finance.

Later on, he will change his mind on these points, but for now he will put them to one side, glancing at them only if he loses his way in the planning. He will now move on to the detail, and will probably use one of the following four main methods. Each of these principal methods has spawned numerous other planning methods. A flow chart, for example, can also be laid out as a 'trickle-down chart'; a spider chart can also be represented as a 'hierarchical chart'. By showing this example, using the four main methods, you will see the principles underlying these ways of planning, regardless of how they have been developed over the years.

● The spider chart

Type of assignment
The spider chart lends itself to assignments which ask you to **create an argument**; they allow for a fluidity of ideas which can be missing from other methods and encourage you to change your mind as you go along.

Writing style
Spider charts tend to encourage a more **discursive style of writing**, with longer sentences, fewer lists, and a more easily developed argument. If your writing style is naturally too note-like, or you tend to cut and paste material for your assignments, you might find this method useful in correcting the problem.

For the example given above, the basic spider chart might look like that shown in Figure 3.

The student has already changed his mind: the advantages of the move will no longer form a whole section, but will be incorporated into the finance section; he has also added a section entitled 'local area' because he realises that he has plenty of information on this, and it will be of interest in considering the move.

This will work as a basic plan, but he needs to develop his thinking about the assignment, and this means making further plans, which will allow him to change his mind again or to work out his ideas in more detail. He might now move on to producing a further spider chart for each section. For the staff section, for example, he could develop his ideas as shown in Figure 4.

The key to a good plan is to change your mind as often as you need to, and this means producing as many spider charts as you need until you feel comfortable. This is, of course, a great work-avoidance scheme, so make sure that you set yourself a time limit for the planning process, so as to resist the temptation to produce the most beautiful plans in the world, without any final product!

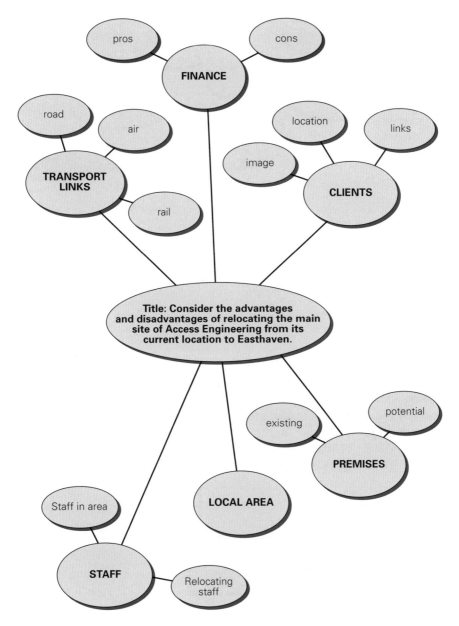

Figure 3

Figure 4

● The flow chart

Type of assignment
A flow chart is a useful method if your assignment is **data rich**, requiring that you give complex information in a logical order, without missing anything out.

Writing style
Flow charts tend to lead to a more **succinct style of writing**, with shorter sentences and paragraphs, more lists and charts and a more linear presentation of material.

   For the example in this chapter, the initial flow chart might look like that in Figure 5. Although this flow chart is organised, and shows a linear flow of information, it is not logical. On looking at it again, the student will realise that finance will need to come either before everything else, or right at the end, as this is likely to be the driving factor

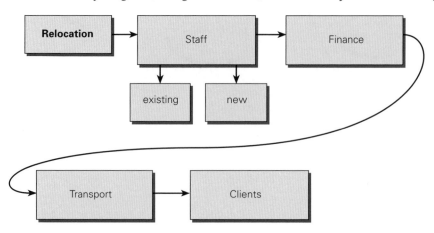

Figure 5

in the relocation. This is the key to working well with flow charts – although they look organised at every stage, you must be prepared to change your mind. You will discover when you try using a flow chart whether this is an obstacle for you; some students find it no problem, whereas others really struggle to see different patterns and possibilities once they have created an initial flow chart.

● The brainstorm

Type of assignment
Brainstorming is not a complete planning method in itself, but is useful for four specific purposes:

1   When you just cannot think how to get started on an assignment and need to loosen up your ideas.
2   When you are working in a group, and want to ensure that everyone is involved in the initial planning.
3   If you find that your writing can get a bit boring.
4   If you think you know about 90 per cent of what you need to say, but cannot help feeling that you have missed a point somewhere.

Writing style
Because brainstorming frees up your ideas, it can also **free up your writing style**, but be careful. Unless you restrain yourself with a more formal planning method in addition to brainstorming, you could be in danger of writing a rather ill-focused assignment.

A brainstorm looks a little like a spider chart, but with none of the connecting lines. Most usually a group of students will work together, passing around a pen and letting each member of the group add an idea in turn. Alternatively, someone might lead the group and add ideas to a flipchart as they come up. Online brainstorming is especially useful if you do not have the time or opportunity to work face to face with your fellow students or tutors. If you have an assignment to master, you can simply set out the broad outline of what you need to do in an email, asking your email recipients to send back very brief emails, no more than a couple of lines, offering you some ideas. In this way you can tap into the expertise not only of your student group, but also of tutors and other experts in your field.

For the example being used here, a brainstorm could look like that shown in Figure 6.

What is achieved during brainstorming is, hopefully, a filled-up and rather messy piece of paper with lots of ideas, some of which will be more relevant than others. The advantage of using this method in this case is that, whilst some of the same ideas have come up, so too have other, less obvious ideas. Nobody has felt responsible yet for creating order out of this chaos, and this has allowed ideas to flow freely. The student will now have to take this plan away and decide which ideas should be kept, and he will

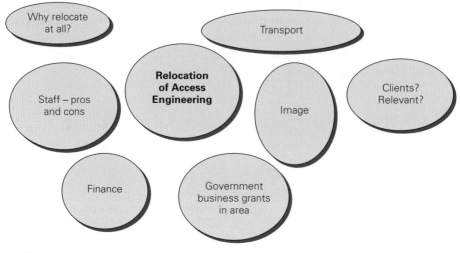

Figure 6

move on to another planning method, using these key ideas to form the framework of the next plan. In this case, it is likely that he will abandon the idea of a full section on government business grants in the area, as he does not have much information on this and feels it could more relevantly be subsumed under the main heading of 'finance'. He will be delighted to have thought of the obvious question 'Why relocate at all?', and may open with this. Because other planning methods would have worked towards organising his data, he could have overlooked this point, yet addressing this fundamental question is a great way to start his essay.

The question mark beside 'clients' highlights another function of plans. Although he will have a remit within which he is working, it is far easier to go back to his tutor with a plan to talk through, rather than just hoping to glean all the instruction and guidance he needs in a more general conversation. In this case he is unsure of whether he is expected to write about the needs of the firm's clients; his plan will show his tutor how this area would fit into his plan overall, making it much easier for them to make a judgement on this together.

● The mind map

Type of assignment

Mind mapping is a very efficient way to **remember concepts and facts**, and as such works well as a revision aid, but it is also a useful method of planning. If you are the type of person who makes a plan and then keeps forgetting to look at it, a mind map will help you to hold the information in your head as you write. It is also a good way to ensure that you work on the essential message in an assignment, rather than getting bogged down in the facts and forgetting the overview of what you want to say. Many educational institutions have mind-mapping software installed on their systems, so it is worth checking whether it is available to you.

Style of writing

A mind map generally takes longer to produce than any other method of planning, and so tends to lead to a more **elegant and persuasive style of writing**. There will be less cutting and pasting and, often, fewer minor mistakes in writing style.

A mind map takes elements of both the spider chart and the flow chart, but you will need to follow several new rules. Whenever you stop on a mind map (each stop is called a 'station') you will need to use at least three colours to illustrate your point – we find it far easier to remember in colour. When you move from a station you can either 'flow', by moving out from the centre in a logical progression, or you can 'bloom', bringing several ideas out from one central point. There are no straight lines in a mind map – everything is written or drawn at eye level and each part of the map joins perfectly onto another part, so there are no random lines which could lead you into forgetting a portion of the plan and having to go back to rewrite sections of your assignment. Ideally, a mind map includes the lowest number of words possible. You are aiming to produce a pictorial representation of your essential message – the facts and figures can be included as you write. Having said that, there is no need to worry if you are not artistic – even the oddest-looking pictures will do; as long as they mean something to you, they have done their job.

As you can see, in Figure 7, this method takes some time. The student has had to decide, at each station, on the best way to represent his ideas and his argument, but

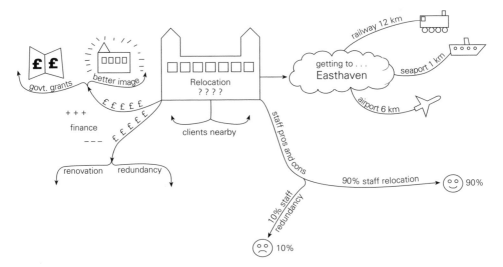

Figure 7

this is actually a benefit. By the time the mind map is complete, he will be sure of what he wants to say and the best way to say it. With practice, a mind map can be a more efficient way of planning than any other method. Mind maps are also an excellent way to record information efficiently. I use them frequently in seminars and meetings, as they allow me to be involved in discussions whilst jotting down a mind map to remind me after the event of what happened. They are much quicker and less distracting than taking notes and can get you a good 'feel' of what happened in the seminar or meeting.

● Return to your six-point plan

Once you have produced a detailed plan, using any of these methods, you will need to look back at your original six-point plan. Even if you have only spent a relatively short time on the detail of your plan, you might be surprised at how far you have moved from your initial ideas. Now is the time to check your progress. Have you abandoned any of your six points? Have you amalgamated any of the points? You now have a last opportunity to add a section to your plan, if you find that you have forgotten any of your initial points; you also have the chance to check your overall structure, to confirm that you have included all of the essential points you need, and that you have left out material that would distract the reader from the main thrust of your argument.

● Add the detail

Many students are happy to write from a diagrammatic plan, and so will start writing at this stage, but others find this confusing, and would prefer to write out a series of headings and subheadings, with bullet-point lists below them. This layout allows you to plan with headings, even if you do not need to include headings in your final written work; it also allows for the addition of notes and timing estimates, and is yet another, final chance to see if anything is missing. For the example in this chapter, the headings have been listed in a report format. You will also notice that a note has been added to the bottom of the plan: 'Signpost timing throughout'. This is the result of an oversight: the student has realised at the last minute that he has not included a section on the timing of the move, but he likes the plan as it is, and is not convinced that this needs to be a major section. So, instead of distorting his outline plan, he has made a note here so that he remembers to mention timing whenever it becomes relevant in the report.

Once you have reached this level of detail in a plan, you can see how easy the writing becomes. You know what material to include and, crucially, you know exactly what you want to say. You will have had the opportunity to share your plan with others, gleaning good ideas as you go along. You may have changed your mind – and so your plans – several times along the way, and will now feel confident about what you have to say

Relocation of Access Engineering

1.0 Introduction
- Background
- Why move at all?
- Can they sell their existing lease?
- Scope of the report   *This section complete by Monday*

2.0 Location, site and services
Size of new site compared to existing site
- Essential services
- Local infrastructure
- **include a map here**   *This section to check in Tuesday's seminar*

3.0 Transport

3.1 Road
- Motorway links
- Main road links
- Problems of traffic congestion

3.2 Rail
- Mainline station
- Light railway links

3.3 Air
   3.3.1 Existing airport links
- Times to major European cities?
   3.3.2 New airport plans
- History of airport plans
- ***include government white paper extract here***

4.0 Staff

4.1 Existing staff
- Relocation of existing staff
- Commuting logistics
- Retraining key staff
- Cost of probable redundancies

4.2 New staff
- Skilled workers in area
- Semi-skilled workers in area
- Cost of training new staff   *To here by Thursday*

5.0 Clients
- Advantages
- ***include benefits chart here***
- Disadvantages
- ***include SWOT analysis here***   *Check this section in study group*

6.0 Finance
- Advantages
- Disadvantages

7.0 Conclusions and recommendations
!!!!MOVE!!!!!!!
- Cost/benefit analysis
- Staff benefits
- Client benefits
- Financial benefits   *Complete by Sunday*

* remember to signpost timing throughout *

and how you intend to say it. Although you will have devoted time to this planning phase, the writing now is going to be easy, and far more persuasive and efficient because you have planned in such detail.

How to progress:

☐ When you attend a meeting or a seminar, spend a few minutes after the event using a planning method to organise the material you have just been discussing. Practising in this way will increase your confidence as you face more challenging planning tasks.

☐ For mind mapping practice, try making a simple mind map during a meeting, or chart the progress of a film you are watching, or use it to replace note taking in a presentation.

☐ To test how effectively you have organised information in the past, look back to an essay, a report or a presentation script/notes you have produced previously, in any context, and retrospectively plan it, using the material within the document and organising it within one of these planning methods. This will reveal areas of weakness in your organisation of material, and give you planning practice.

5 Writing Essays

Essay writing will become a regular part of your life as a student, and as well as being used for assessment purposes, essays are useful learning activities in themselves.

During my time as a student I came to enjoy essays not just for the process of proving my learning and sharing my ideas, but because they were the most tangible product of my hard work. I seemed to spend so much time taking in information and trying to figure things out that it was a relief to finally be able to write something down for someone else to read, even though this meant that I had to face the anxiety of waiting for a result once the essay was marked. Essays allow you to see that you are making progress, and looking back on essays gives you a sense of where you have been and how far you have come.

For mature students the very thought of an essay can be daunting in the early stages of study. If you have been out of education for a time you might feel that your essay-writing skills have become rusty; if you are used to producing professional documents such as reports, you might struggle to adapt to this new way of expressing yourself. If you are undertaking a distance or e-learning course, you might feel isolated in this challenge.

● Knowing what you are being asked to do

The first thing to work out is what an essay title is actually asking you to do: the words used in the title are crucial. Table 4 shows some of the most **common keywords** used in essay titles.

● Making a plan

Once you know what is expected of you, you can begin to plan your essay. A plan can make so much difference to the quality of your writing, and it will also speed up the writing process: once you know what you want to say, writing it is far easier and quicker.

A key thing to remember, as has already been mentioned in the 'Planning' chapter of this guide, is that you cannot make more than **5–7 main points** in anything you produce. This might sound like very few points, but it is just the way human beings work – we really can't cope with more than this number of points. That is why a traditional

Keyword	What you are expected to do
Compare	Highlight similarities (and perhaps differences) and, sometimes, offer a preference for one option or another.
Contrast	Bring out the differences between two topics, or two aspects of a topic.
Discuss/Consider	This is the widest possible instruction: you will be considering several aspects of the topic, and perhaps developing an argument.
Examine	This is generally a little easier. You are being asked to look in detail at the topic, but will not necessarily be expected to develop an argument.
Explore	This is similar to 'examine', except that you will range more widely, but still in great detail.
Describe	This is very specific, and you must follow the detail in the title carefully to make sure that you only describe what is relevant.
State	This is usually used for briefer essays, where you will be describing something (usually a series of facts) but in a less extended way than if you were asked to 'describe'.
Analyse	This requires you to divide a subject up and look at each part of the topic in an analytical way. This is often used to evaluate several options given in the title.
Explain	This is similar to 'analyse', but usually with a sense that you are looking at one process or area of a topic, rather than dividing it up into many aspects.
Trace	This is often used for factual essays, where you are describing something, aiming to explain how something has developed.
Outline	This is similar to 'trace', except that you are usually covering a broader topic. You are being asked to make general points about an area.
Summarise	Here you are being asked to bring a subject under control, to show your understanding of the topic by being able to put forward its key points briefly.
Evaluate	This one is tricky: rather than being tempted to describe the topic, you are expected to use your knowledge to make a judgement about a topic or an opinion.

Table 4

play structure has five acts; it also is why politicians try to cover no more than this in speeches. If you are writing a dissertation or a lengthy essay, you might have many minor points under each of your main points; if you are giving a ten-minute presentation you might only try to cover three or four points, but the general principle remains the same.

Let's look at this in practice. For the rest of this chapter I will show you how you might work on an essay entitled:

'Discuss the problem of global warming, analysing its probable causes and considering possible solutions to the problem.'

You will notice straight away that several keywords are being used in this title, as is often the case. You have a wide opening option, as you are asked to discuss the problem. This allows you to range quite widely at the outset. You are then being asked to become more analytical, to evaluate the facts and come to some conclusion about 'probable causes'. Finally, you are asked to consider 'possible solutions' – you are not expected to provide the last word on solutions here, but instead to write about different possible options.

So, this will be an essay in three parts, with each part serving a slightly different function. You will have beside you in readiness any notes that you have made from seminars, lectures and textbooks in preparation for the essay, but you need at the outset to write down your first 'gut reaction' thoughts about the essay. These might be:

1 Controversy – is it anything to do with us, or just a natural event?
2 Greenhouse gases cause the problem.
3 Rainforests could help to solve the problem.
4 Climate change has happened before – ice ages and warm periods.
5 Problems of industrialisation.
6 Private consumerism might only affect it marginally.
7 Statistics can be confusing – or deceptive.
8 Makes climate warmer, but also shifts weather patterns in a good way.
9 Rising sea levels as a result of glaciers melting.
10 Are we powerless? Is it just the problem of big business?
11 Carbon trading – will it work?
12 There might be bigger problems which we should fix first.
13 Freak weather conditions in the UK in last five years – flooding etc.
14 What can we do as individuals?
15 Communication between big carbon-emitting nations is vital.

By this stage I have hit a problem. Having said that the essay should cover 5–7 main points, I already have 15 points and I haven't even begun to look at my notes yet. The solution to the problem is simple – I just need to take the material to the next level, by grouping points together so that they fit within 5–7 main points.

In this case, I could rearrange the material to look like this:

Is it a problem?
1   Controversy – is it anything to do with us, or just a natural event?
2   Statistics can be confusing – or deceptive.
3   Climate change has happened before – ice ages and warm periods.

The problem we can see ...
4   Freak weather conditions in the UK in last five years – flooding etc.
5   Makes climate warmer, but also shifts weather patterns in a good way.
6   Rising sea levels as a result of glaciers melting.

Causes of the problem ...
7   Greenhouse gases cause the problem.
8   Problems of industrialisation.

Possible solutions ...
9   Private consumerism might only affect it marginally.
10   Rainforests could help to solve the problem.
11   Communication between big carbon emitting nations is vital.
12   Carbon trading – will it work?
13   Are we powerless? Is it just the problem of big business?

Where next?
14   What can we do as individuals?
15   There might be bigger problems which we should fix first.

I have now rearranged my thoughts so that I have five main points: the first four address the title in the order in which it is written; the last one lets me range a bit more widely at the end of the essay, if I have the space. Although there are five main points here, other points may arise as I come to do a more detailed plan, which will include the material I have gathered in my notes.

A spider chart at this stage will help me to expand on my points and to include information from my notes. The spider chart for this essay could look like that shown in Figure 8. It would give me a good idea of the areas I want to cover in the essay. In reality it is likely to become far more complicated, with many more bubbles, but this will suffice here.

Now that we have worked through the planning for this example, you might like to try it for yourself. On your next essay, try using the two blank charts provided in Tables 5 and 6 to help you get your material organised. The first will contain your initial thoughts; in the second you can order your thoughts by arranging them into 5–7 groups.

Figure 8

Essay title:	
My first 'gut reaction' thoughts on points to include in the essay	
1	
2	
3	
4	
5	
6	
7	
8	
9	
10	
11	
12	
13	
14	
15	
16	
17	
18	
19	
20	

Table 5

© Lucinda Becker (2009), *The Mature Student's Handbook*,
Palgrave Macmillan Ltd

Essay title:	
Group 1	
Group 2	
Group 3	
Group 4	
Group 5	
Group 6	
Group 7	

Table 6

© Lucinda Becker (2009), *The Mature Student's Handbook*,
Palgrave Macmillan Ltd

Now you are ready to work through your notes from lectures and texts to make a more complex plan, using the groups in Table 6 as your main points on the blank spider chart provided (Figure 9). You will probably need to add more bubbles to this spider chart as your plan becomes more complex. It would be possible to write your essay from the spider chart, but you may prefer instead to list all of your paragraphs, with bullet-point notes of what you intend to include in each section.

● Beginning to write

The worst thing about essay writing is undoubtedly the blank piece of paper or blank computer screen that faces you before the first sentence. These can reduce even the most experienced writer to a jibbering wreck before a single word has been achieved. Suddenly, the urge to clean out the kitchen cupboards, or meet a friend for coffee or even deflea the cat can seem overwhelming. Detailed planning is one way to ambush yourself: once you have immersed yourself in your plan, the piece of work feels almost written in your mind. If you can get up a good head of steam in the planning stage, you can fool yourself into beginning to write almost without realising it. This is the most efficient way of coping with the problem: to move straight from planning into writing – you can go back to the plan to check it after you have written the first couple of paragraphs.

Of course, this type of ambush is not always possible, and you can find yourself with writer's block. This is both frustrating and confidence sapping, as you feel powerless to remedy the problem and the prospect of writing seems overwhelming. If this happens to you, you might like to try one of the tricks I use:

- Write the first few sentences in pencil – that way it won't feel as if you are producing anything important or permanent, which reduces your anxiety level.
- Put your ideas for the first few paragraphs into detailed bullet-point lists – just expanding each bullet point into a sentence or two seems far less daunting than starting from scratch with complete sentences.
- Without looking at your plan, write a brief summary of what you want to say in your assignment. At the least, you have begun to write; at best, you might have just written a brilliant introduction by mistake.
- Keep a permanent document in your computer entitled 'rubbish'. Begin to write your assignment in that document, then take a break and look at it again. You might be able to cut and paste some of it across into your assignment, banishing the blank page without any great effort.

By planning well, not only will you be encouraging yourself to write, but you can also avoid a common pitfall in essay writing. Unless you are specifically asked to do so, or you really think it is essential to what you are going to say next, don't waste time (and valuable space) simply giving lengthy definitions of the words in a title. The essay

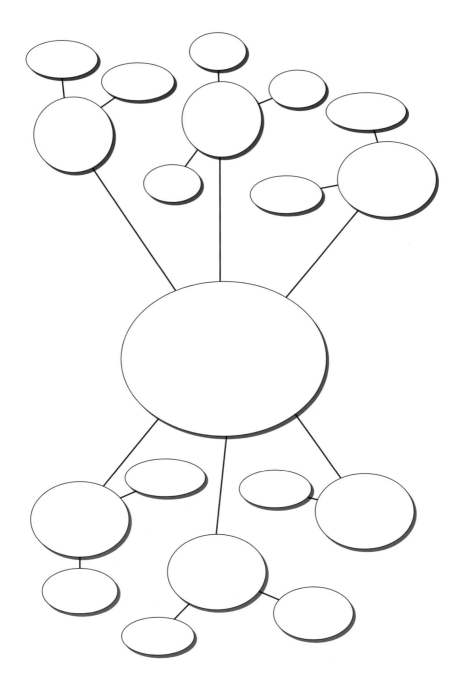

Figure 9

marker will assume that you know what the words in the title mean. You might want to start with one or two concise quotes to show your knowledge of the area, but this is usually all that is necessary.

Students are sometimes advised to write their introduction only when they have completed the rest of the essay. I would argue against this approach. Planning is not just about organising material: it is about thinking through your topic until you have a clear idea in your mind's eye of how the essay will 'look', its shape and the ways in which it will persuade the reader. The point of having a really good plan is that you know exactly what you want to say before you begin to write, so that the writing process is easier and you have the mental space to think about the more refined aspects of presenting your argument. An introduction is a good way to test this. If you can write your introduction first, without any great problem, you know that your plan is sufficiently detailed, and that you have given the topic enough thought to write easily and persuasively.

Your structure will be dictated to some extent by what you have to say, but the same principles apply to any essay. Each box in the following pages contains a section of the example essay, with the first sentence of each section and then notes in italics.

● Paragraphs, signposting and persuasion

Although the detail of writing (punctuation, formal expression, grammar and vocabulary) more properly belongs to another book, it is worth mentioning here three aspects of essay writing which can cause a particular problem for mature students – using paragraphs and signposting to help your reader through your essay, and writing concisely yet persuasively. Confusion can arise in these areas because mature students have experience of other types of writing, which make different demands on their skills, or because it has been some time since they wrote in such a formal, academic way.

The answer to the problem comes from the thorough planning discussed here, but also from work on **paragraphing** and **signposting**. Well-ordered paragraphs are essential if you are to produce an impressive piece of work. Any marker who sees an essay with hardly any paragraph breaks will approach the work with a heavy heart – there will be no sense of order, no way to put the document down for a moment to think about a point, no persuasive structure. If you are unsure about paragraphing, then make clear in your plan what you intend to include in each paragraph and, if you are in doubt, include extra paragraph breaks rather than fewer.

Good paragraphing links to the second structural option you have for impressing the marker: signposting. This is a simple enough concept, but students sometimes find that they are hardly signposting at all. A brief description of the method should be enough to get you going on it.

Signposting relies on two things: the way you 'package' your paragraphs and sections and the words that you use. You will see from the example opposite that I have told the reader what to expect in each section, and I would close each section by

Introduction

(I have included headings here, but these would not necessarily be included in the final essay.)

D.C. Larnes has defined global warming as 'an irreversible change in weather patterns which results in higher global temperatures, a dramatic increase in freak weather conditions, such as flooding and drought, and an inevitable – and disastrous – rise in sea levels globally'. The effects of global warming, as defined in Larnes's work *Dying Earth: Our Legacy*, are many, and it could be argued that we are seeing all of them in our world today.

List here some of the effects of global warming.

The World Health Organization recently issued a statement on global warming which seems to make the position clear: 'global warming is the single largest threat to our society today. Unless we act now, and act decisively, our ability to fix the problem in the future will be far outweighed by the cost of coping with the damage it is causing'. Clearly this is a problem which should be addressed, and in this essay I will be considering the probable causes of global warming and some of the possible solutions to the problem, and will conclude with an analysis of whether we should devote a huge amount of global resources to trying to halt or reverse the situation.

Against Global Warming

Before considering the causes of global warming, it is worth noting that, despite what seems at times to be overwhelming evidence, there are still those who argue that it does not exist in the way that we have come to think of it; that scientists have exaggerated the problem, or that it is a natural rather than a man-made problem which will reverse itself over time. Whilst T.S. Polik claims that it is 'a man made Armageddon', L.B. Jarvis claims that 'it is a hoax, no more than a blip in our weather patterns. It will right itself, but before that happens it will continue to grow as a key cause for western angst. We will pour billions of dollars into the problem, at the expense of other far more pressing global disasters'.

List here the arguments against global warming, but keep it brief so as not to spend too much time on an argument that goes against the premise of the title.

Causes of Global Warming

Despite such debate over global warming, most scientists seem to agree that it is a real phenomenon, and that it is, partially if not necessarily wholly, caused by human activity.

This section will run to several paragraphs, each one considering a different cause.

Solutions – Global

If global warming is caused principally by industrialisation, consumerism and globalisation, it makes sense to look first for global solutions to the problem.

There are two 'solutions' sections here, as this is a major part of the essay and it would be easy to become confused in this central section. This section would run to several paragraphs, outlining global responses to the problem.

Solutions – Individual

The solution to the problem of global warming rests not only with global companies and governments, but also with individual actions, although how great an impact any of us can make is open to some debate.

This is also a major section of the essay, but here the analysis would become more of a debate, with individuals' actions being assessed for their impact on the situation. The section would conclude with the assertion that individuals can make a difference.

Is It Worth It?

It is clear, from the evidence discussed here, that solutions to global warming – even if only partial solutions – can be found at both the global and the individual level. However, some critics argue that this is not the direction in which we should be looking at all. H.D. Hickson states quite categorically that 'global warming and climate change generally is the biggest white elephant in recent history'. His argument rests upon the fact that, for every dollar spent on preventing or reversing global warming, the same dollar could be much better spent on the prevention of HIV/AIDS, or vaccinations against childhood diseases in Africa. This is a hugely contentious area, and is worth some examination here.

You will not want to dwell too long on this issue, as it might take your focus off the main premise of the essay, but it would be worthwhile to devote a paragraph or two to this viewpoint, to show that you have researched all aspects of the topic.

Conclusion

Global warming is a complex issue and scientists are still debating both its causes and potential solutions to the problem. It is clear that, at both the global and the individual level, we can make a difference. The debate at this stage is one of prioritisation, of how much we should do and whether it is to the detriment of a global effort to solve more pressing problems in the world today.

You will notice that this is a very brief conclusion, and this is often best. A lengthy conclusion can confuse the reader, making it unclear as to whether you are really offering a conclusion or still debating the arguments. It should be the case that, if you have produced all of your evidence, and made your arguments effectively, a conclusion needs to be no more than an affirmation of what your reader has already concluded.

reiterating, in just a sentence, the point that I have just been trying to make. This is good for me, because it will be very obvious to me when I do this if I have failed to really make any point at all in a section. It is also good for my reader. The sentence won't make my point for me in its entirety, but it will alert the reader if the point wasn't clear before, and encourage the marker to read the section again with that point in mind.

Once you have mastered the structure, you will need to start including signposting words. These are words that do not add anything to the substance of what you are saying, but do tell the reader how to approach a sentence or paragraph. Key signposting words appear in Table 7. The tick boxes will give you the chance to check back through your last essay to see if (and how) you have used any of them.

All these signposting words and phrases help your reader through your work. This is to the good, but you also need to make your writing as fluent and clear as possible. This requires a good use of vocabulary, punctuation and grammar, but it also relies on your being able to say what you want to say **succinctly** and **persuasively**. It is not unusual for mature students to approach me in some frustration, because they have written 1200 words of a 2000-word essay and realise, to their horror, that they have only covered the first of six main points that they were hoping to make.

There are several solutions to this problem – better planning and making lists of exactly what you want to say in each section of an essay will help, as will jotting on your plan a rough indication of how many words you expect to need for each section. To make your writing forceful, it is also a good idea to see all of your writing as made up of either '**power**' words or '**paste**' words. The power words convey your essential message, and the paste words expand on this, adding descriptive, signposting or connecting words. We need both power and paste words, but in the right proportion.

An example here will help to make this clear. Below is a fire evacuation instruction, written in far too rambling a style:

> 1. If you notice a fire, however large or small, please leave the room in an orderly fashion. 2. You may take your personal belongings with you, but if you leave anything behind, try to remain calm and do not return to the room under any circumstances. 3. To do so would be a disciplinary offence. 4. Instead, try to remain calm and proceed to the Assembly Point to await further instructions from Dave.

This does not read like a fire instruction; it sounds more like a chat about what we might choose to do if a fire broke out. Therefore, it has failed in its main purpose, but let us look to see why it has all gone so wrong.

Sentence 1: the writer is already confused – how can it matter whether the fire is large or small? Sentence 2: an unnecessary option is given: now I am worried about taking my belongings with me. I wouldn't even have thought to do this, but the writer has now told me that I can, so my focus is on that option, rather than on leaving the building. Sentence 3: as if aware that the writing is rambling, the writer changes tone completely. From being a friendly little chat, this has now become an overly official document. Sentence 4: who on earth is Dave? The fire marshall perhaps? And where do

Signposting words and phrases	What they signal to the reader	✔
Whilst, whereas, although	I am about to tell you something, but you have to read to the end of the sentence or paragraph because I am going to go on to challenge or modify the point I have just made.	
Therefore, in conclusion	This is a key sentence to read if you are going to understand me. Once I have said this, I will either have finished the essay, or I will move on to my next main section.	
Claim	I am not convinced by what this person has to say, so I will be quoting or outlining the point, but I will go on to dispute it in some way.	
Fact	This is a fact that we must both accept if we are to agree on the direction of my argument. (This is a very strong signposting word – be wary of using it unless you are absolutely sure.)	
To conclude	I am at the end of my essay – read this last bit carefully because I am going to sum up my argument in just a few sentences.	
It seems likely that	It doesn't seem likely to everyone, but for the moment let's assume that it is the case that the points I am about to make are reliable.	
It is easy to assume, we might assume	I am not going to assume for one moment. I will tell you what a less informed person will assume, but then I will qualify the points so as to make them clearer.	
However	You have to read on now – whatever I have said in my last sentence or paragraph is important, but you can only fully appreciate it if you read to the end of this section.	
Despite	I have made a point, and you could think about that, but now I want to move on to my next point.	
To make my point more clearly	I am confused – I am not really sure of the point I am trying to make, so I will have another stab at it here (try to avoid ever using this one!).	

Table 7

I meet him? Where is this Assembly Point? Aware that the notice has gone on too long, the writer is now being far too brief.

The instruction could be far more helpful if I took out the paste words, the rambling, and included a greater proportion of power words:

> In the event of a fire, leave the building and go to Assembly Point B, in Courtyard 4, to await instructions from a Fire Marshall. Do not return to the building until you are told it is safe to do so.

This is much better – it tells me clearly what I need to do, does not give me confusing options, and it is authoritative without being bullying.

Of course, I could write the instruction with nothing but power words, in which case it would read like this:

> FIRE??? LEAVE!!!

This would make my point, but would be like shouting at the reader, and would hardly be reassuring.

You are trying to find a balance between paste words and power words in your essay writing, and the exercise below will help you to discover whether you are a natural rambler or naturally too brief in your writing style, which will allow you to modify it if need be. This piece of writing is very rambling, with far too many words for the main points that the writer is trying to make:

> However hard I try, and believe me, I have tried very hard, I simply cannot get my poor, muddled old head to understand the rules of English grammar. It is a totally arcane system of largely irrelevant and redundant rules, completely useless to the average essay writer. In addition, I am much afraid to say that this particular writer has never had more than the most meagre grasp of what is going on when it comes to most punctuation. Having said that, I have no intention of giving in: oh no, that is not my way at all. I will conquer grammar. It is my firm intention, and I am not easily cast aside in these things, to master the semi-colon by the end of next week, even if it kills me, which, in all likelihood, it will. Nevertheless, despite the earnest and, at times, pathetic pleas of my family and friends, I will succeed. I never give up lightly. To be able to achieve this almost Herculean goal will be a source of inexpressible joy; to fail would plunge me into unmitigated gloom. (186 words)

Of course, I hope you don't feel this way about grammar. What we get from this piece of writing is a clear sense of how the writer *feels* about the subject, but far less of an idea of what point is actually being made.

Before you check the answer below, take a few minutes to underline all of the words in this passage which you think are power words – those words which are essential, and must be included if we are to understand the main point of the piece.

Now check below: the underlined words (just 16 of them) are the power words:

However hard I try, and believe me, I have tried very hard, <u>I simply cannot</u> get my poor, muddled old head to <u>understand</u> the <u>rules</u> of <u>English grammar</u>. It is a totally arcane system of largely irrelevant and redundant rules, completely useless to the average essay writer. In addition, I am much afraid to say that this particular writer has never had more than the most meagre grasp of what is going on when it comes to most punctuation. Having said that, I have no intention of giving in: oh no, that is not my way at all. <u>I will</u> conquer grammar. It is my firm intention, and I am not easily cast aside in these things, to <u>master</u> the <u>semi-colon by</u> the <u>end of next week</u>, even if it kills me, which, in all likelihood, it will. Nevertheless, despite the earnest and, at times, pathetic pleas of my family and friends, I will succeed. I never give up lightly. To be able to achieve this almost Herculean goal will be a source of inexpressible joy; to fail would plunge me into unmitigated gloom.

You would not want to write with no more than power words, of course. You would need to put back the connecting words that make our language make sense. Apart from the word 'simply', there is very little indication in these power words as to how the writer actually feels, but these 16 words do tell us the problem and what the writer intends to do about it.

Now that you have completed this exercise, go back to your own writing and check a section of it for power words (you will need about three pages of writing). This is an art, not a science, but you need to be able to justify to yourself the proportion of paste and power words in the writing. If you have relatively few power words, is this because you are using paste words to be persuasive? Is this working?

Once you have mastered the essay, you will feel more confident in your strength as a student, and will be happier about expressing your views in other arenas, such as presentations and your dissertation.

For most students, an essay is the first product of their studying, and you are likely to view yourself differently once you have passed this milestone. You have something to show for your work, and you will begin to see how your written output fits into an overall scheme of studying. Make the most of this milestone, and the ones to come: keep copies of your essays to hand throughout your course, not just so that you can check back to them for revision or future assignments, but also to remind yourself, if your energy or motivation is flagging, that you have produced something tangible and that you will go on to produce much more.

How to progress:

- [ ] Show your essays to non-specialist friends or family. They will enjoy learning about what you are doing, and they will point out any inconsistencies in your style and the organisation of your material; they will also be able to confirm how easy it is to follow your argument. As non-specialists, they will also ask any obvious questions which you have overlooked.

- [ ] Study skills advisers at your institution will be of particular help to you here, both in person and in print. Guides to essay writing should be available to you in hard copy and online.

- [ ] Websites away from your institution can be useful, both for advice and for showing you examples of essays and how they are structured, but *be careful*. Avoid anything that looks even remotely like a cheat site, and never assume that the facts within internet essays will be accurate. Academic journals also offer useful examples of how material in your field might be organised, and are more reliable as to fact.

6 Presentations

When I came to give my first presentation as a mature student, to my regular seminar group, I did not anticipate having any great problem with the task. I had talked quite happily in the seminar and I was keen on the subject of my presentation. I was enthusiastic about getting my points across. So how, I asked myself afterwards, did it all go so very wrong? What had been a perfectly adequate ten-minute presentation in my kitchen magically reduced itself to a six-minute rant in the seminar. What I thought were finely honed points of interest, receiving due emphasis in rehearsal, seemed to become garbled in the telling. Where I thought I might engage my audience, I ended up engaging the seminar room floor, which is where I seemed to be looking for most of the presentation.

Of course, it probably wasn't as bad as my memory told me it was, but it did teach me a valuable lesson about presentations: I just did not know enough about how to do them, and nothing was going to replace experience, which is the key ingredient to successful presentations. I couldn't have given myself more real-life experience, but how I wished I had rehearsed to more than my kitchen sink, more than once. If I had taken a more structured approach to the process, such as I have outlined below, I would not necessarily have been a brilliant presenter, but I would have been a far better presenter than the one I was that day.

Seminar presentations (discussed above in the chapter on seminars) are just one form of presentation that you might be called upon to give as a student. Others might include:

- a research presentation;
- presentation of the results of laboratory work or a project;
- a dissertation presentation;
- a conference paper;
- a professional presentation.

A **research presentation** is a way of showing how far you've progressed in your area of study. It is often quite a formal presentation, given to a panel of experts, but its goal is to be of benefit to you. You are laying out your ideas, and the experts are there to give you advice and support.

Presenting the **results** of laboratory work or a project might be a formal occasion, but you have the advantage of being very sure of your material, as you may have been working on it for some time. This type of presentation is sometimes an end in itself (that is, you are marked on your performance), but sometimes it is a way of marking your progress, and in this case you will be expecting feedback and guidance.

A **dissertation presentation** is either given at the end, or more usually towards the beginning, of the dissertation process. If it is a final dissertation presentation, it serves to show off your knowledge and you will not be expecting guidance, just a grade. In this case your presentation is a way of supporting what you have written in your dissertation. If the presentation is at the outset, it will feel much more like a research presentation, with a panel of experts advising you as to the best direction for your research. You will not be expected to be an expert in the field, just to have given some thought to how your dissertation might progress.

Giving a **conference paper** might involve giving a presentation, but more often it is very different from a presentation, in that you are required simply to read the paper you have prepared for the conference: no visual aids, no need to stand up, no need to interact with the audience (beyond smiling and making eye contact) until the end of the paper, when you will be answering questions; this is the moment when your presentation skills will matter.

Many students do not expect to give a **professional presentation**, but if your course of study is linked to your workplace, your employer might expect you to share your knowledge with your colleagues; if you are on a placement you might also be called upon to give a professional presentation. Similarly, if you are using your new qualification to try to get a new job, or a promotion in your existing organisation, a professional presentation might be needed. You might also be called upon to give this type of presentation if you are contributing to a conference that does not stick to the traditional academic line of contributors 'giving a paper'.

It is tempting, when you are given a presentation task, just to get on with it, to begin working on your material and planning the presentation structure. It is far better to take a step back first, and check that you know as much as possible about the task before you plunge in.

The following is a list of things to check:

- What type of presentation am I to give? Which of the descriptions above best describes it?
- Do I have to produce my own title, or will it be given to me? Is there any way I can change it as things develop?
- How long have I been given for the presentation? Is there any leeway?
- What is the structure of the presentation? Is my time divided between giving the presentation and taking questions? Is there to be a discussion afterwards that I will be expected to lead?
- How many presenters are speaking on the same occasion? Where am I in the running order?
- Is this a stand-alone presentation, or are they being grouped, so that I will have to know who else is speaking on a similar topic and talk to them about how we can work together?

- If this is a group presentation, do I have the contact details of every other speaker in my group?
- What is the presentation room like? Large, small, hot and stuffy, breezy, noisy? Can I alter the conditions (windows, air conditioning, lighting and so on)? Can I alter the layout of the room on the day, even between presentations? How much time will I be given to set up?
- What visual aids can I use (overhead projector, data projector, demonstration area, slides, DVD or video and so on)? What is expected of me? What is everyone else likely to use?

Presentation techniques

Before considering the content of your presentation, it is worth checking some general points of presenting, to make sure that you are in the best position before you start, and to give you the chance to work on these techniques as you prepare.

Controlling your nerves is always going to be important in presenting, but one myth must be dispelled first: good presenters are not those students who breezily assure anyone who will listen that they never have an attack of nerves, that they can give a presentation with no notes and no nervousness. Long experience has taught me that these students are, almost without exception, poor presenters. Feeling nervous about a presentation is always, without doubt, a good thing.

Of course, you won't want your nerves to overwhelm you on the day, and there are plenty of relaxation techniques you can try, but these only work well if you first follow the golden rule of presentations: prepare thoroughly and **rehearse adequately**. It goes without saying that presentations get easier with practice, so try to volunteer for as many informal presentations (seminar presentations, speaking at small student events or in discussion groups) before you have to face a formal presenting situation.

Breathing should be the most natural thing in the world, but it is a surprisingly difficult thing to keep doing when you are nervous. You will find that your mouth has gone dry, that you speed up each sentence, that you suddenly take a huge breath at the wrong moment, and that you feel exhausted at the end of a presentation. This is all linked to poor breathing. Students sometimes say that they can hardly remember breathing at all during a presentation – this is because they took many shallow breaths and a couple of huge breaths, rather than breathing steadily throughout. The great thing about controlling your breathing is that you can fool your brain into believing that you are less nervous than you are, so you produce less adrenalin and you find, miraculously, that you actually are less nervous.

Presenters are sometimes advised to take a few deep breaths before they get up to speak: this is not always a good idea – it can make you feel quite faint as you flood your nervous body with oxygen. Instead, the secret is to breathe from your diaphragm rather than from your upper chest or back. Put your hand on your **diaphragm** (the central soft muscle just below your rib cage) and relax. You will find that your diaphragm moves a little each time you breathe. Breathe out naturally, and simply close your mouth. Keep it closed until you really feel the need to take a breath (you should feel as you do when you have been under water for too long). This is the important bit: don't actively take a breath, which will use the intercostal muscles in your back and raise your shoulders, but simply open your mouth. Your diaphragm will instinctively take over and you will feel it 'pop out' as the breath comes in. This technique takes some practising, but once you have mastered it, you will be able to breathe well throughout a presentation and keep your voice (and your nerves) under control.

The **speed of your speech** is natural to you: some of us speak too fast, some too slowly. However, in a presentation it is very uncommon to speak too slowly; nerves speed up our speech. You might want to work on slowing your speech down (it should feel a little unnatural for you if you are speaking at a good presentation pace) and it is a good idea to rehearse with a colleague, so that you can have somebody listening to you from the back of the room, reminding you to speak up, or to slow down. For many of us, especially if we do not give many presentations, it is difficult to slow down our speech entirely. If this is the case for you, you can try a method that allows you to stick more closely to your normal speed of speech, but still allows the audience to understand what you are saying. This is to halt, deliberately, between each sentence. This tiny pause gives the audience the chance to process what you have just said, even if you said it a little too fast. Ideally, you will be able to slow down your speech altogether, but working on both slowing and pausing is a good way to make sure that you get your message across effectively.

Silence might not be the most obvious component of a presentation, but in fact there is an enormous amount of silence in any good presentation, and you have to make it happen. You will wait for silence (or as near as you can get to it) as you smile at the audience and wait to begin your presentation; you will allow for silence as the audience looks at your visual aids; you will leave tiny pauses after giving facts and figures, and perhaps at the end of each sentence; you will create silence as you smile at the audience when you make a particularly interesting point; you will endure the silence as you wait for questions at the end. The ability to cope with silence marks out an effective presenter, so make sure that, as you rehearse, you deliberately allow for silence, and time your presentation accordingly. It takes some nerve to do it, but it is well worth the effort.

If you have a regional **accent**, or if English is not your first language, you might be concerned that the audience will struggle to understand what you have to say. It is unrealistic to expect that you will change your voice pattern entirely for a presentation, and it would not be a good idea even if you could achieve it: we all enjoy hearing different accents, and they add interest if yours is one in a series of presentations. If you expect this to be a problem for you, make sure that you employ the technique of pausing after each sentence or cluster of sentences, so that the audience's ears can catch up with you. You can also usefully change the emphasis of your visual aids. Rather than just showing slides that give the detail of the presentation, include slides which give simple outlines of what you are about to say next. Audiences cope well with accents if they know what to expect.

Body language has become a popular subject in recent years: you can buy any number of books on the subject, and it is fascinating to be able to 'read' the people around you. To be an effective presenter you do not need to study body language to this level of detail; you just need to be able to control your body on the day. The one piece of body language that you must always ignore is shaking. Most of us shake when we are nervous, and some of us shake out of all proportion to the nerves that we feel, but an audience will never mind about you shaking. You might want to employ some tactics to minimise the effect of shaking (such as never holding up a piece of paper, avoiding using a laser pointer which will also shake, wearing trousers rather than a skirt so that nobody can see your hemline shaking) but actually audiences tend to respond to shaking positively. It shows that you are taking this seriously, that you are determined to share your ideas despite your nerves, and, of course, audience members will be pleased that you are the one shaking, not them!

Once you ignore the fact that you might shake on the day, you will be free to focus on the aspects of body language that do matter. Although there are a multitude of body language signals that you could work on, the most important are listed here:

- *Smile* – as often as you can. If you smile at the beginning of a presentation, this is entirely to your benefit. The audience will instinctively smile back at you, so you will be faced at the outset with a sea of smiling faces, rather than an anxious-looking group. Smile again at the end: it is a clear indication to the audience that you really have finished your presentation and that you are ready for questions. The most difficult time to smile is if things go wrong, but if you smile when you drop your note cards, or click onto the wrong slide, or muddle your words, the audience will automatically feel protective towards you, and will smile back supportively.
- *Present to the audience, not to the wall.* Always make sure that your toes are pointing towards the audience. That way, you will avoid slowly turning to face the screen on which you are presenting slides, or facing a side wall rather than the audience.
- *Avoid fiddly or repetitive body language.* When you rehearse, do it at least once in front of a friend, if you can. This way you can ask your observer to check whether you have any irritating nervous habits (rocking or swaying back and forth, fiddling with your hair, rattling the change in your pockets, slouching down on one hip and so on) and you can make a positive effort to eliminate this negative body language.
- *Stand unsupported.* However great the temptation, avoid leaning on a chair or lectern, or half hitching yourself onto a desk. It is comforting to have some-thing to lean on, but you risk making your presentation look too casual, and your body language can seem very awkward to an audience, even if you feel comforted by it.
- *Only point out the obscure.* Try to avoid pointing to every line on a slide, when the audience can perfectly well read what you have to say; equally, if you have

a complicated diagram, try only to point to those sections of it that the audience might find difficult to grasp, otherwise you risk looking as if you are not sure of what is on there yourself or, even worse, you might seem to be doubting the audience's ability to understand the obvious.

The **layout** of a room and the **equipment** you will use can be surprisingly tricky unless you rehearse with them in mind. Decide on how you want the seating to be arranged (a horseshoe shape to encourage discussion, rows of seats for a more formal presentation) and be prepared to change the layout before your presentation. You will not want to have everyone moving desks and chairs in the moments before you speak, but a visit to the room earlier in the day will allow you to check the layout and, if it is possible, to change it to suit your presentation. The most important points about the room will be its temperature and light level. Open the windows if there is a break before your presentation, to make sure that the audience does not feel sleepy from lack of fresh air, and work with the light level you have. If you can see slides without dimming the lights, this will be better than having to fiddle with the lights during the presentation.

Equipment can trip you up and this is a waste of your nervous energy. **Rehearse with the equipment** you will use, and master it before the day. Always assume that it might go wrong, so have back-up ready (a video of a demonstration in case it fails at the crucial moment; overhead projector acetates or handouts in case your slide show fails on the day). Keep your slides clear and simple – smaller than a 20-point font will be difficult to see, as will the colours red, orange and yellow. An extract from a book or article, or a web page download, is only worth showing for its general layout; there will be too much detail for the audience to take in on screen, so a handout for this would be better if you need to tackle the detail. Remember to include some slides which give the basics of the presentation: your name, the title of your presentation and the overall structure of what you want to say.

Checklist 4 will help you to prepare for your next presentation.

● **Preparing your presentation**

As you work on your material, take the following factors into account.

Give yourself enough **time** to prepare well. Presentations often work best when you have time to prepare the material in advance, then take a break of a day or so before you rehearse the presentation and rework the material, then take another break before you begin on your final rehearsals. In this way you allow your mind to assimilate the material, to grasp the shape of your presentation and to consider, without you consciously working on it, how best to present your chosen material. Although this means working on the presentation earlier than you might have expected to, it does tend to save you time overall and give a better effect. Cramming too many last-minute rehearsals into your schedule can lead to a rushed or too stilted style of presenting.

CHECKLIST 4

	✔
I've worked on my nerves so that I have them under control, even though I still feel nervous in a good way.	
I have worked on my breathing techniques and can now breathe from my diaphragm.	
I have rehearsed with a friend and know that I speak slowly enough; I have mastered the art of pausing for a moment between sentences or clusters of sentences. I have marked pauses on my cue cards so that I won't forget on the day.	
I have an accent but am still clear in my speech, *or* I think my accent could cause a problem so I have put in place techniques to overcome this.	
I have worked on my body language and put reminders on my cue cards to smile, and to turn back to the audience after I have shown them a slide. I have moved every tempting surface out of my way in the room so there is nothing left on which I can lean or slouch.	
A friend or tutor has watched my presentation and has pointed out my distracting body language habits; I have rectified them ready for my presentation.	
I have checked the layout of the room and made arrangements to change the layout on the day to suit my needs. I know how to dim the lights, change the air conditioning, close the blinds and open the windows.	
I have checked my slides in the available light level and know whether I have to dim the lights or close the blinds for part of my presentation. If this is the case, I have enlisted the help of a colleague to do this for me so that I remain focused on my presentation.	

If you are giving a group presentation, **communication** between the group is going to be vital. Make sure you can contact everyone – perhaps set up an internet group – and decide at the outset who is tackling which section of the presentation. You might want to put your strongest speaker first, or have your weakest speaker take on a smaller task, such as introducing the speakers and the topic and fielding questions at the end. Being clear about who is covering what, and how, will save you time and trouble later. When setting the timing of meetings and rehearsals, be clear about when you will have the time to focus on the presentation, and when your time will have to be given to other tasks. Arrange to have one rehearsal very early on, as soon as you have pulled some

© Lucinda Becker (2009), *The Mature Student's Handbook*,
Palgrave Macmillan Ltd

sketchy material together, so you can get an idea of how the presentation will work as a whole before you spend too much time polishing up your material.

A **script** might be a good way to start your rehearsals, but aim to abandon this in favour of cue cards after a couple of practices. Reading from a script rarely makes for a good presentation. It might help you to time your material and feel more confident about exactly what you want to say, but it will force you to talk too quickly and in a monotone expression if you use a full script on the day. The example presentation given here will show you how to move from a scripted talk to an effective presentation.

Example presentation

For the purposes of this example, let us assume that a mature student, studying a course in engineering, construction management or public finance, has been asked to present on the following topic:

'Should the private sector be involved in the funding of major public construction works, or should they be funded solely by the government budget?'

The first thing the student would do is to check the basics: the timing of the presentation, its structure, whether it is a group or single presentation, and the equipment available. Then he will produce a spider chart to organise his ideas, as shown in Figure 10.

If the student feels confident about the subject matter and has plenty of presentation experience, he might move straight from this plan to producing overheads and cue cards for the presentation. For the less experienced student, there is an easier and more reassuring way to proceed, and this is to produce a script in the first instance. The advantage of this approach is that it allows you to see the shape of your entire presentation before you begin to work on the timing, and it allows you to practise from the script for your first rehearsal, which will boost your confidence.

For this presentation, the opening of the script might read like this:

> *Hello. My name is Michael Fenton and my presentation today concerns the funding of essential infrastructure. I will be looking at the advantages and disadvantages of both private and public funding and drawing conclusions from my research. I hope to show that it is possible for private and public funding bodies to work together to minimise the problems and maximise the benefits of the system. ***intro slide****
>
> *The project I intend to focus on is the building of the Kenton toll bridge, 32.8 km north of Stourchurch and 6.5 km west of the coastal village of Bridestow. ***slide of map*** When the project was first proposed in 2006, it was to be funded from central government funds, but the government announced that a report produced by Greenpeace (Eastern region) had caused a delay. However, at the time it was suspected that finance was a key factor in postponing the project: moreover, a change of government caused further delays.*
>
> *The Kenton toll bridge project is now going ahead, funded by a partnership*

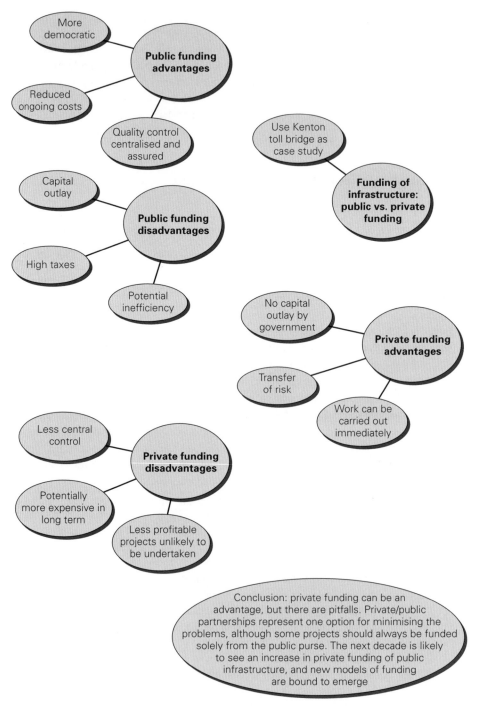

Figure 10

between government and private industry, and it offers an example of how partnership funding can work. Before I look at this project in detail, I would like to consider the benefits and potential pitfalls of private and public funding in a range of infrastructure projects. ***slides showing structure of presentation***

This script is full: it even includes the speaker's name, but this is a good idea. Many students forget to give their name at the outset of the presentation: you might assume that the audience members will know your name, but some won't, and it helps to settle you (and the audience) down if you introduce yourself and your presentation in this way. This script includes plenty of detail, but it cannot work as a presentation, partly because there is too much detail, but also because the words used are written English, not spoken English. The student needs to abandon words and phrases such as 'moreover' and 'I would like to consider ...', unless these are natural to his speech patterns. By moving away from the script he will keep his presentation fresh and interesting, as the words and phrases he uses will be those that enter his head at the time, rather than those he has used again and again in rehearsal.

So, now he must move his presentation from a script to **cue cards**. These cards (4" × 6" index cards are useful for this) have several benefits: they give him something to hold on to whilst he is talking, to stop him fiddling; they are easy to read at a glance so that he does not lose his way; and they can include cues to himself that he could not so effectively include in a script, or on his slides.

The secret to success with cue cards is to put as little information as possible on them: they should not simply replace the script word for word, but should be prompts to a more natural style of speaking. The cue cards for the section of the presentation above could look like this:

Hello. My name is Michael Fenton and I am looking today at the funding of essential infrastructure.

Public/private partnerships can be a good thing.

Using my research.

Presentation lasts 20 mins.

Q & A for 10 mins.

SMILE!!   1

Kenton toll bridge ⟶

~ 33 km north of Stourchurch

6.5 km west of Bridestow

SHOW MAP   2

2006 – first proposed – public funded.

Delayed – Greenpeace – financial problems really?

Change of govt.

SLOW DOWN   **3**

Before detail, look at advantages and disadvantages of public and private funding.

Talk through presentation structure from slides.

TWO STRUCTURE SLIIDES   **4**

All of these cards are sparse – any more detail on them would encourage the speaker to read them as if from a script, and if he lost his place he could easily become confused. The cards are intended to be glanced at as reminders only; his rehearsals will have left him feeling confident enough to fill in the gaps.

You will be amazed at how much more competent you become, and how much more confident you feel, after just a few **rehearsals**. You need to aim for at least six rehearsals: see Checklist 5. Not all of us are naturally brilliant presenters, but we can all deliver an effective presentation if we take control of the material and work to persuade our audience. The combination of methodical preparation and structured rehearsal outlined here will give you the best possible support for your presentation.

Learning to give successful presentations is about more than simply completing a task well: it can have a profound effect on your view of yourself and your studying. In a presentation you stand alone, on an island of your knowledge, looking across at your listeners and aiming to convince them of your point of view. You only have to achieve this once and your confidence in yourself and your mastery of your subject will soar. Being able to articulate your thoughts well, under pressure and within time constraints, will be one of the most useful skills you learn as a mature student. Often a good presentation is the 'point of no return' for students: once you have done this well, you cannot imagine giving up on your studying.

CHECKLIST 5

	✔
Rehearsal 1: from your full script, checking that you have enough, but not too much, material for the time allowed.	
After this rehearsal: cut down or add to your script so that it fits the timing.	
Rehearsal 2: again from your full script, checking that the timing is now right.	
After this rehearsal: make final changes to your script in the light of your timing ⟶ reduce your script to cue cards.	
Rehearsal 3: working from your cue cards, check the timing again.	
After this rehearsal: remove cue cards to extract sections of the presentation if it is taking too long.	
Rehearsal 4: again, working from your cue cards, rehearse while thinking now about your body language and incorporating your visual aids to check on the time.	
After this rehearsal: rework your cue cards, making sure that they are as sparse as you can make them whilst still containing the essential details. Add prompts to yourself to slow down, or pause, or smile in some sections of the presentation.	
Rehearsal 5: this is your final run-through to check on timing and delivery. By now you will feel confidence in your material, and changing slides or pointing out the detail on them should feel natural.	
After this rehearsal: mark up some of your cue cards as 'timing markers', noting on them that you are halfway through, or ten minutes in, or five minutes from the end.	
Rehearsal 6: try to rehearse now in front of at least one colleague; ideally arrange for a group of you to rehearse together. See this as a dress rehearsal, and ask your colleagues to point out any problems with the content, the timing, your voice or body language, or the clarity of what you are trying to say.	
After this rehearsal: hopefully there will be nothing to do after this rehearsal, except to await the presentation, knowing that you are nervous but confident in what you have prepared. Too many rehearsals can leave your presentation feeling stale, so only rehearse after this stage if your 'dress rehearsal' threw up specific problems on which you need to work.	

© Lucinda Becker (2009), *The Mature Student's Handbook*,
Palgrave Macmillan Ltd

How to progress:

- [ ] Even if you are not giving a group presentation, it is a good idea to find a presentation partner, someone who will watch you rehearse and give you feedback, on the basis that you will return the favour.

- [ ] If you can keep the same partner over the length of your course, you can remind each other of how well you have progressed, and your partner can remind you, each time you prepare a presentation, of little faults that you are trying to eradicate.

- [ ] Having a 'plant' in the audience is always a good plan. This supportive audience member might do nothing more than smile encouragingly, but he or she will also have a good question ready to ask if a deathly, prolonged silence arises at the opening of the question-and-answer section of the presentation.

7 Writing Reports

The planning method you use for a report need be no different from your usual essay planning method, but you will need to plan very thoroughly, as you will have to decide in advance exactly where in your report each section of material will be included. There are two areas of reports that tend to trip up students: **layout** and **decimal notation**, and each of these will be covered here.

● Report layout

Although some departments and subject areas will deviate a little from the standard report layout, knowing how the structure should work in a standard format will give you a good grounding, especially if you are asked to write a 'freestyle report', where you can decide on the best structure to use. Below I have listed the sections of a report, in the order in which they are usually arranged, and the options you have about what to include in each section.

A standard report structure looks like this:

- Title page
- Acknowledgements
- Summary
- Table of contents
- Introduction
- Main body
- Conclusions
- Recommendations
- Appendices and annexes
- References

The **title page** of a report is the page that makes the document look like a report. As well as the report usually being bound in some way, the front page is distinctive because it is the most creative page: this is where you might include your institution's logo, or a mission statement, or a picture of some sort. This is all optional, of course, but what will always be included on the front page are your name (and perhaps your student number), the date of the report, the title of the report and any administrative details (such as 'confidential' or 'submitted as dissertation project' or the names of the intended readers). Sometimes these administrative details are included on the back of the front page.

It is a nice idea to include **acknowledgements**, thanking all those who have helped you to produce the report. Just one word of caution: make sure that these people want to be thanked. This might seem strange, but there are occasions when people would rather not be thanked. For example, if you have included the material of others in the report you will, of course, reference this in the report, but if those people do not agree with your conclusions, or have had no time to read the report, then they might prefer not to be thanked in the acknowledgements in case readers assume that they do agree with everything you have written.

The **summary** of a report is intended to work as a stand-alone document. That is, any reader should be able to read the summary and understand all the essential features of the report. So, you will need to include an outline of why the report has been written, details of where the evidence came from (although you will try to avoid including detailed evidence in the summary) and a brief synopsis of your conclusions and recommendations. The summary should be as brief and inclusive as you can make it and you will usually be given guidelines as to how long it should be for your report. An **executive summary** tends not to be included in academic reports as this is a summary produced just for the executive board of an organisation: it is shorter than a standard summary, giving only the briefest outline of the content of the report, focusing on the conclusions and recommendations. An **abstract** differs from a summary in that it is usually intended to be used as a search document for electronic databases, or as a 'taster' at the beginning of a report or an article. It usually has a strict word count (200–300 words is common) and may be made up entirely of keywords for search engines to find, rather than summarising the report in its entirety.

Because reports do not usually have indexes, the **table of contents** is vital. Readers will use this to search the report and decide which sections to read, so you need to include in the table of contents all of the headings, even the most minor ones. As well as the headings in the report, you might also include in your table of contents a list of the appendix material, and a list of all of the graphic items (graphs, charts, maps and so on) in the report.

I have listed the **introduction** as a separate item here because, although it does form part of the main body of the report, some institutions choose not to have this as a numbered heading. Your introduction will usually give the background to the report (that is, an introduction to the project you have carried out, or the subject area you are covering), the scope of the report (the way in which it is intended to be read and used) and any restrictions on the report (that is, the areas you are not covering, and why). The heading 'Introduction' might be replaced by another introductory heading, such as 'Background'.

In the **main body** of the report you will include all of your evidence. It will be divided into as many sections as you need to cover your subject area, with headings and subheadings (see decimal notation, below). As this frequently confuses students, it is worth pointing out that there is never a heading in a report actually entitled 'main body' – this is just a way to describe the central section of your report.

The **conclusions** section of a report is always written like this, in the plural, even if you are only drawing one, single conclusion from your evidence. This is to distinguish between an essay, where you come to a conclusion (that is, the end of the essay) and a report, where you are drawing conclusions from the evidence. You will not include any evidence in the conclusions section and you might find it helpful to make a bullet-pointt list of your conclusions before you go on to talk about them in more detail, to help the reader to follow your train of thought, and to remind you of where you are going as you write. In some reports the 'Conclusions' section might be replaced by a section entitled 'Discussion' or 'Results'.

A **recommendations** section is not always needed in an academic report. If you are including recommendations in a report you might find it difficult to separate these two final sections, and it is perfectly acceptable to have one section entitled 'Conclusions and recommendations', although you will often find that, once you have written the report and come to check it, you can see things more clearly and can separate the sections at that stage.

Appendices are perhaps the most useful part of the report for a student, as they allow you to escape from a too rigid word count. Reports should be accessible and easy to read, and this is achieved by appendices. In the report itself you are developing an argument, seeking to persuade your reader of something. You will include essential evidence in the report as you go along, but place back-up evidence in appendices, so that none of your research is wasted (although do make sure that your reader understands the relevance of the material in appendices). The way to decide whether to put material in the report itself or in an appendix is to put yourself in the reader's place. You include in the report any evidence (a section of a map, for example) that is of immediate use to the reader in understanding a section, whilst the background evidence (the entire map) would be placed in an appendix. Appendices are especially useful for material to which you know the reader will have to refer frequently throughout the report. It is fine to repeat material: for example, to include a graph in the report itself in an early section, but then also to include it as an appendix because you are referring to it intermittently throughout the report.

An **annexe** is similar to an appendix. An appendix is a document that you can paginate yourself, so the page numbers of your appendices will run sequentially with the rest of your report. An annexe is a document that cannot be numbered by you (for example, an instruction manual from a manufacturer or a government white paper). These will be listed in order in the table of contents, but without page numbers.

The **references** section is, in one way, the same as a bibliography section in an essay. You will reference all of your sources just as you would in an essay, both those from which you have quoted directly and those which you have used for your research in preparing the report. You might also include other reference documents. These might include a glossary (which is usually the very last page, or can be placed within the introduction), a schedule of work still to be carried out, a table of weights and measures – in short, anything that will be of general use to the reader in approaching your report.

● Decimal notation

This can be a confusing concept at first, but actually it is surprisingly easy (and extremely useful) once you get used to it. The idea behind decimal notation is that it organises the material perfectly; as a result, every single heading in a report is given a number that denotes the level of the heading (that is, the relative importance of the material in that section).

Imagine that a student has been on a two-week placement during a course of study. On that placement the student is asked to carry out a study of the website of the organisation, and make recommendations for a new design, and is also asked to redesign the internal newsletter to staff. During the placement the student will have made notes and gathered material as the tasks were carried out. The structure of the main section of the final report (excluding title page, appendices, table of contents and so on), including decimal notation, will look like this:

1.0   Introduction
    1.1.   The placement organisation (its function and output)
    1.2.   The placement details (when, how long)
    1.3.   The projects
        1.3.1.   The website project (succinct outline of the brief)
        1.3.2.   The newsletter project (succinct outline of the brief)
    1.4.   Scope of the project (time limitations and so on)

2.0   The website project
    2.1.   Current website design (including printout of home page)
    2.2.   Issues to consider in redesign
        2.2.1.   Company logo
        2.2.2.   Use of colour
        2.2.3.   Font options
        2.2.4.   Content
        2.2.5.   Structure of whole site
    2.3.   Research into websites (looking at competitors' websites)
    2.4.   Market research amongst clients
        2.4.1.   Rationale for email survey
        2.4.2.   Headline results of email survey
        2.4.3.   Analysis of results
    2.5.   Suggested new website options

3.0   The newsletter project
    3.1.   Current newsletter layout and content
    3.2.   Potential problem areas

➡

Two things emerge from this layout. The first is that the student has decided on the focus of the report (looking at the projects, rather than focusing on the career development aspects of the placement) and, as importantly, a 3000-word report has just been transformed into a task based on many much smaller sections: this is much easier to tackle.

The challenge in using decimal notation is that you have to decide in advance exactly how important a section of material is, and where it will fit into the report; the payback is that everything is perfectly in place before you have written a word of the report. The result is that you have the mental space when you are writing to think about how you are expressing things and to consider the detail of grammar and punctuation: you will be clearer in your purpose and more persuasive in your writing.

How to progress:

☐ Decimal notation is the aspect of report writing which usually concerns students most. Try taking any document you read apart by listing the headings you would use to organise the material, and using the decimal notation system to organise the headings. This is relatively easy in a well-written academic document – for more of a challenge, try doing it for a magazine article or a chapter from a book.

☐ Take any opportunity you have to look at other people's reports, and be critical in your analysis. Try to identify where the argument is weak, or the writing is less than persuasive, or the organisation is muddled. Seeing weaknesses in reports around you will give you more confidence when you come to write your own.

☐ If you find the rigid structure of reports difficult, try imposing a report format on every plan you make. It makes no difference that the final product – essay, presentation, seminar session – will not be presented in a report format; the practice will have been useful to you.

8 Writing a Dissertation

The title 'dissertation' can cover several different projects: you might produce a dissertation as the culmination of a course of study; it might be the result of a discrete work-based project or a purely academic project; or the writing up of your professional experience and development during your course of study. Whatever its basis, it will always involve a level of independent research, it will usually be a major part of your course, and it will be part of your life for weeks or months. It can seem overwhelming in prospect: this section is designed to make the whole process easier.

Many students take an unproductive attitude to their dissertations, and it is easy to see why. At some stage all students come up against a block in their progress. Either they start early, feeling in control and ahead of their colleagues, and then slow down dramatically after a few weeks, or they put off beginning until the last possible moment, and then rush through in a haze of panic. Both of these approaches are the result of a general anxiety about the scale and importance of the task, which seems to loom larger every time you contemplate it.

In rare cases a student might feel initially that the word count is not enough; in most cases, however, the word count is seen as daunting and unmanageable, particularly if you have been producing relatively short essays or reports for the rest of your course. Although students invariably say that the word count, in the end, was not enough, and that they would like to have written much more, this is of little comfort to you when you are worrying about how to begin, how to structure, how to write. Telling yourself that it is only four or five essays' worth of writing helps a bit, but you will still be aware in the back of your mind that this is something different, not just some essays strung together but an extended piece of independent research and writing.

● Supervision

Of course, 'independent' does not mean 'alone'. You will be allocated a supervisor for your dissertation, and the supervisory role will be crucial. There are some key questions to consider at the outset:

1   Why this supervisor? Does your supervisor have a special interest in your dissertation topic? How might this help you?

2   Familiar territory? If you have worked with your dissertation supervisor before, you will already be familiar with the ways in which you work together. This can

be an advantage, but make sure that you still take stock of this new situation and relationship by considering the questions here.

3   When is your supervisor available? Dissertation topics are often decided months in advance of the deadline. You will need to make sure that your supervisor is available when you need help, rather than being away from your place of study, perhaps on research leave. If this is the case you should be allocated a new supervisor, but this is worth knowing in advance, and you might want to make your plans around your supervisor's availability.

4   How often will your supervisor expect to see you? There is no right or wrong way to supervise any student, and supervisions will vary in length and frequency as your work progresses. Use your personalised timetable (see Ch. 11) to ensure that you work with your supervisor as much or as little as fits your needs.

5   Is there a protocol? Have you been given deadlines for your dissertation development, such as a deadline for producing a detailed plan, or a first draft? These deadlines are usually a good guideline as to how best to approach the work ahead of you, and your supervisor will expect to work within these unless you have a pressing reason not to comply: communication is essential here.

6   How should I communicate with my supervisor? This is going to be important, especially as your relationship develops. Discover whether your supervisor prefers to be contacted by phone, or email, or would prefer always to work face to face.

7   Prepare for each supervision. There is never enough time to say everything you want to say in a supervision, either for your supervisor or for you, but you can overcome this challenge by emailing material in advance of every supervision. You might want to send your supervisor a copy of your personalised timetable, your rough plan for a dissertation section, a first draft of a section or a list of questions you want to ask. This will make your time together more productive.

8   After each supervision, email your supervisor to confirm the points which were discussed and agreed. This way you both have a record of events, and your supervisor will have the chance to reflect upon your progress, and the opportunity to come back to you with more ideas.

Although you will want to follow the advice offered by your supervisor, you also need to take some control of the relationship. Your maturity will work to your benefit in making the relationship work.

● Timing

You already know how you work best: either **slow and steady**, ticking off a list of accomplishments as you go, or **fast and furious** in a last-minute dash to the finishing line. There is no need to change the way you work – and there is very little point. If you suddenly decide that your natural working style will not suit the production of a dissertation you are likely to feel uncomfortable with your new way of working throughout the process. Instead, try not to become concerned with how anyone else works – you know how you work best, and this is always going to be the most productive method to take, as long as you **work with your supervisor** to guarantee the finished product is delivered on time and to the standard you want.

● Word count

Usually a dissertation is between 8000 and 15,000 words long, and usually there will be an allowable leeway of ten per cent on your given word count. Whatever the word count, you are very unlikely to find that you have too few words, so it is safe to work on the assumption that you are going to be cutting words out at the end rather than trying to find more. This is handy, as editing is a far easier – and more productive – process than adding more writing. Editing down the number of words in the final polishing of the dissertation challenges you to be more focused and more succinct, which in turn will produce a more thought-provoking and authoritative piece of writing.

● Title

You will probably find that you begin with a **topic area** or a draft title, which will have to be narrowed down as you begin to work through the research. By doing this, you become more focused about what you want to explore and much firmer in your ideas about what is relevant to your hypothesis. (By the way, 'hypothesis' is just an academic way of saying your central premise, the points you are trying to make, the theory you are trying to prove, the argument you are trying to develop.)

With this thought in mind, try not to become too attached to your title. It is not intended to be set in stone; it is just a working outline of where you might go in the coming weeks and months. As your thoughts develop and your research deepens, you may well change your draft title, but this is not a sign of indecision – it is a clear signal that you are mastering your subject.

● Openings and endings

When you are planning your dissertation, it is a good idea to allocate an approximate word count to each section. This might change, but it will alert you to problems of overrun before they become too serious. There is a temptation to give too many words over to the introduction and the conclusion of a dissertation. In the best dissertations, these sections tend to be quite brief – an authoritative overview of what you intend to do, and how, and why, with a clear outline of the areas to be covered, is enough for the introduction.

If you keep your conclusion brief in terms of what you say about your completed research, it will allow you to pose some further questions, to indicate how your research might have developed had you had more space, to show where more research is needed in the future, and why. This is always an impressive way to end, as it proves that you have not tired of your subject area, and that you are aware of its potential for future study.

Students are often encouraged to write the introduction to their dissertation last, on the principle that by that stage they will know what they want to say. This can be a good thing, but it is worth considering the advantages of writing it earlier. If you write your introduction last, it can be difficult to remain concise, and all too easy to find yourself trying to rewrite the entire dissertation. If you write it first, even in draft form, from your detailed plan, this can offer two benefits. Firstly, it keeps it brief, as you are at the stage of taking an overview without all the detail (just as your reader will be at this stage of reading the work). Secondly, it allows you to test your detailed plan. If you find that you are struggling to think how to phrase what you want to say, or you are finding it impossible to be clear and concise, the chances are that your plan needs more work, and it is better to know this at an early stage, before you try to write your later sections.

● Motivation

You can expect to hit a slow period in your dissertation preparation at some point, and this is normal. What you want to avoid is allowing this minor break from the work to become overwhelming, so that you find it increasingly difficult to return to the project, and begin to resent the imposition it seems to be placing on you. The way to avoid this potential problem is to keep writing – anything. Write synopses of the texts you have read, write a list of the next texts to read, write down your thoughts on how a chapter might develop, write a more detailed plan – really, anything at all which makes you feel that you are making progress and working on the dissertation. That way, even when you have a less productive period, you will not feel as if you have abandoned it altogether.

● Subject matter

Almost without exception, dissertation topics narrow as the work progresses, and this is as it should be. You will want to keep a balance between the general (an overview of your area), the specific (the examples you intend to analyse in more detail) and the analytical (the hypothesis you are testing, the argument you are developing). The easiest way to do this is to think at the outset of **research questions**. What questions are you trying to answer? These may not be included in your title, but they will be pivotal to your success.

The example I will use in this section is the case of a financial markets student considering the impact of the internet on the retail market. Her first research question is actually her draft title: '*What has been the impact of the internet on the retail market?*', but other research questions are also implied here:

- 'Is the internet a good or a bad thing for retail trade?'
- 'In what precise ways has the internet changed the pattern of buying and selling?'
- 'How might this impact alter over time?'
- 'What factors might cause the future pattern of internet trading to differ from that which we see today?'

She could add many more questions to this list, but already it has become clear that, whilst the initial idea is a good one, it needs to be narrowed down. She cannot cover all of this ground in a 10,000-word dissertation (nor could she, indeed, in a 20,000-word dissertation). As is so often the case, the student has stumbled on a subject which could happily occupy a doctoral student for three years or so, and so she begins the process of narrowing by interrogating the premise of her original questions:

- What do I mean by 'the internet'? This is far too large a term – I will just look at one internet seller, Amazon.
- What do I mean by 'retail trade'? This is too vague – I will restrict myself to the sale of books on Amazon.
- Where is the retail trade? I cannot cover the whole world – I will look only at the impact of Amazon in the UK.
- What do I mean by 'the pattern of buying and selling?' – again, this is a bit vague – I will keep an eye on this to see if I can define it more clearly in the planning stages.
- What do I mean by alterations over time? I might be interested in the whole history of Amazon, but I will keep this to a brief overview. I will look at the effect on specific groups, such as consumers, Amazon itself, and retailers of various sorts.
- What do I mean by a 'good or a bad thing for retail trade'? This could be my hypothesis – that Amazon has had an effect on the book trade in the UK, and this could be either a good or a bad thing.

Now she has some more realistic research questions, and her title (which she might change again later) is: '*Has the emergence of Amazon in the UK been advantageous or detrimental for the retail book trade in the UK?*' This is a sharper and far more focused title, which can reasonably be addressed in her 10,000 word count.

The six points of her initial plan are now clear:

1   Look at Amazon – a brief view of its history and current position.
2   Look at the benefits to Amazon of its emergence in the market.
3   Look at advantages and disadvantages to different types of bookseller.

4   Look at benefits and pitfalls for book buyers.
5   Look at the UK economy.
6   Look at creativity – is this development good for authors?

It is clear that the first two points of her plan will be relatively straightforward, whilst points three to five might each split into several different sections. Her last section is perhaps a little whimsical, but she feels that it might give an interesting lift to the end of the dissertation. She is aware that she might change her mind on these points, but is now in a position to make the spider chart shown in Figure 11. It would not be possible to write an entire dissertation from this plan, and the student is aware that she will have to produce several more detailed plans for most sections.

● Planning

Even if you are not a natural planner, **a dissertation has to be planned**. There are several reasons for this:

- An unplanned dissertation tends to become four or five connected essays, because it is just too large a piece of work to see in your mind's eye in its entirety unless it is planned.
- A plan allows you to discuss your dissertation in detail with your supervisor.
- Although you might not expect it, your planning method will have some effect on your style of writing, which will be especially useful to you if you are naturally too concise or too rambling in your writing style.
- Any tutor can spot an unplanned dissertation a mile off! Even if you have all the material you need, and have good points to make, an unplanned dissertation results in your marker losing faith in the work.
- A plan is not simply a way of gathering material together in an organised way: it is part of the thinking process, and so ensures a more authoritative end product.

This last point is the most important. Ideally, you will make many plans for your dissertation as your thoughts develop. You might have detailed plans for each section and an overview plan. You will, hopefully, change your mind, and thus your plans, several times; by the time you start to write it up, this should be the easy bit. You will know exactly what you want to say, you will be confident about your conclusions and you will have the mental space to consider how best to write, because the planning has finalised how the dissertation will develop.

Figure 11

● Research and writing

Just as your plan will now be built around your research ideas, and the narrowing down of your sphere of reference as you interrogate and refine those ideas, so too should your research activities and your writing up hang off your plan. You will still be writing something during this time, of course. As I suggested earlier, you will be producing synopses of the research material you have mastered, or writing up notes on texts, or working on a more refined plan.

You might also be producing a **research notebook**, which is a great way to avoid the feeling that it is all cramming in on you, that there is too much to do and that the whole project is getting out of hand. A research notebook is an A5, hardback, lined notebook in which you can jot down any research ideas you have. You might already have a similar reading notebook, with the texts you intend to study for your dissertation safely stored there; your research notebook will be a way to contain your research ideas.

As with a reading notebook, this will be a working guide, and it will save you from the pitfall of thinking that every random thought you have is vital to your dissertation and so should have an impact on your plan. Every time you think of a research area, or you have a supervision, or you read some new material which includes novel concepts, use your research notebook to capture your thoughts. When you are working through your plan for a section, you can look through your research notebook and decide whether, on reflection, any of these ideas should be included, or should influence the pattern of the plan. Looking back like this, perhaps some weeks after you jotted down an idea, will give you some perspective, and allow you to judge whether the idea is a good one, whether you have the space to include it, and whether it can be incorporated into your existing plan or needs a new section of its own. If the idea were in a plan and then abandoned, you might lose it forever; the huge advantage of a research notebook is that it allows you to make judgements, to choose which ideas to develop and which to leave alone, but the idea is never lost – it sits in your research notebook, waiting for a time when you might want to revisit a subject area.

A research notebook for the student whose dissertation we are examining in this chapter could look like that shown in Table 8, once she has looked back over it and made her judgement on the value of each entry.

Your research notebook will not end up looking quite like your reading notebook. There, you will be aiming to have studied, or examined and rejected, all of the texts listed. Here, you will inevitably have some ideas which remain good thoughts, but which you do not have the space to develop fully in your dissertation, or thoughts which will take you off at too much of a tangent. These are the thoughts which you stow away, ready for your next assignment, or perhaps they are the ideas which will help to influence you in choosing your next module, or an entirely new course of study. Just as the notes you make in this guide will form a record of your thoughts, feelings and ideas during your study, so too will your research notebook remain as a record of your progress, and perhaps a guide to parts of your future.

Not enough space?	Are CD sales affected in the same way as book sales?
Use in introduction	Check out comparative sales figures of Play.com and those of Amazon
Only if time at the end	If Amazon's sales are levelling off, does that mean there is a new retail trend somewhere that I should mention?
Check with Dr Scully – maybe for next project?	What about creativity in self-authored books sold through Amazon marketplace – would be good to find an example?
Use in Section 2	Check out Tesco sales of books – maybe compare to a small, independent bookseller over the last five years?
Is there any easily accessible info on this? Check back to retail trends lectures	Would it be worth looking at how fast, and how big, high street booksellers took to selling on the internet – did any resist? Why? What happened? Why didn't Waterstones set up their own internet site? Why join with Amazon?

Table 8

Writing up your dissertation should be delayed until you have a detailed plan and feel fairly comfortable that you have done enough research to support it. This might be a detailed plan of the entire dissertation, or just one section, but the writing method should be the same: try to write the section you have planned in one go. This will make for a more elegant style of writing and will help you to retain your overview of where you are going.

Students are sometimes told that they should read a written assignment through twice, checking for errors. This is actually the worst way to find mistakes – it is boring, and you will be reading the document as its writer, not as a reader. You need to alienate yourself from the text, to become a reader, if you are to find the errors. Part of this technique will come from leaving your work for a while (as long as you can within your schedule) and returning to it afresh; and part comes from working through it systematically but not simply reading it through. Instead, try this double-checking method:

First check: spellcheck one last time, then go through the entire document at some speed, fast enough that you cannot read entire sentences, slow enough that you can get a sense of the shape of the document. As you go through, have a red pen beside you and mark in the margins the initials that show where changes need to be made:

- If you are including appendices, have you put all the necessary material in appendices, or are there sections where the material in the main body of the document is too dense, and should be relegated to appendices at this stage?

(Put a big, red 'A' in the margin next to these sections, then keep going at the same, brisk speed.)

- Does the introduction match the main body of the document? If you wrote the introduction first, did you later include a new section of material which you should now mention in the introduction?

(Put an 'I' in the margin next to these sections and move on.)

- Does all of your formatting still work? Has the font size on one of the subheadings changed for no apparent reason? Did you change your style of labelling or bullet-point lists from one section to another?

(For any stylistic problems such as this, put an 'F' in the margin before moving on.)

- Is everything clearly labelled? It is easy to forget to label a chart, graph or image, particularly if you have pasted it into the document or added it at the last minute.

(Put an 'L' in the margin for these mistakes.)

- Have you included enough 'white space'? Readers need white space if they are to find your document accessible and persuasive. This means always double spacing, leaving plenty of space around textual inserts such as charts and diagrams, and making sure that there is a good break between sections.

(Put 'WS' in the margin where you think you could insert more white space to good effect.)

- Does it 'dip' towards the end? This is the only time in your first check that you will slow down a little. We all tend to lose concentration about three-quarters of the way through a document, so you will want to check this section more slowly – not with a view to reading every word, but on the lookout for glaring errors.

(A red line in the margin will show you where these errors have crept in so that you can go back to them later.)

- Are you being nice to your reader? It makes sense not to alienate your reader (who in most cases will be your marker as well) with mistakes that can easily be eradicated. As you go through, try to notice any jargon you have used which might not be understood by a reader (remembering that second markers or external examiners will not necessarily be experts purely in your field), or any acronyms that you have included but not explained. Look for anything at all, in fact, which might make your reader struggle to appreciate your document.

Now that you have worked through briskly and found structural errors, you will be in a position to correct these before you move on to the second check. The first check will only have taken minutes, but it will successfully have moved you away from the text as a writer, and helped you to see it as a reader. Once you have corrected any errors, try to leave it alone for a while again, so that you can regain a distanced perspective on it.

Then, move on to the **second check**:

- Logical ordering? I am still not suggesting here that you read through the document in its entirety. Instead, turn first to your table of contents or your overall structure. Now that it is written in full, does your order still seem logical to you? This is the point at which you might cut and paste whole sections so that your work flows more easily.
- Summary inclusive enough? If you have included a summary, you are now in a position to check whether it is comprehensive, covering all of the major points which you have made later in the document.
- Summary brief enough? This is a pleasurable task at this stage: working through your summary to make sure that you have made it succinct, comprehensive and elegant.
- Projection of objectivity? This involves looking again at the overall structure. If you are creating an argument based on evidence, have you looked at both sides of the argument throughout? This might involve a little rewriting as you insert a brief section to demonstrate that you are being objective.
- Conclusions clear? Now move to the end of the document to make sure that you are clear about your conclusions, and that your reader will have no problem following you through the document to the conclusions you have drawn.
- Details check. Only at this point do you work through the document once, straight through from beginning to end, to check for typing errors and other mistakes. You should only need to do this once, and although you will be checking meticulously, it need not take long as you have already done so much preparatory work. I would advise against checking it through in detail more than once. You are unlikely to find many mistakes on a second or third reading, and you are more likely to begin to change your mind and start fiddling unnecessarily with the text. It helps at this stage to read the work out loud to yourself, so that you can hear mistakes and tone problems.
- Tone checked? As you carry out this final check, always have in the back of your mind the issue of tone. Did you sound unnecessarily anxious somewhere? Or hesitant for no reason except that you were tired when you wrote a

section? Did you feel very emotional at any point? (You will have made more mistakes in that section.) Does your tone let you down anywhere? It is surprisingly easy to write in a way that sounds bored, or pompous or confused, even if you felt none of these things, so make sure that there is a 'tone checker' in your head before this final check through.

It might seem as if I am suggesting a lot of hard work here, but in fact this two-stage method of checking is both more productive and faster than laboriously and rather passively reading a document through twice, and once you begin to find mistakes you will be inspired to keep going.

Throughout this chapter on dissertations the key has been one of containment – containing your ideas in such a way that they do not run away with you; containing your plan so that it does not become too huge; containing your work rate so that the process remains methodical and productive.

What will make your dissertation so significant to you is the fact that it is likely to be the single most important piece of work you will produce, and the one of which you will be most proud. You will probably have it bound ready for marking, so that it looks like a book: mine still stands on my bookcase and occasionally I notice it and smile. It was hard work, it is far from perfect, and I wish I could rewrite it now that I understand more of my subject, but it was the one thing that truly made me feel that I had 'arrived' as a successful mature student.

How to progress:

☐ A dissertation is not really like four or five essays strung together, but it is a little like a book, which is why the sections are often called 'chapters', even if they are only a few pages long. With this in mind, you could begin to look critically at books you are reading – both fiction and non-fiction – to see how authors create connectivity between chapters and how they develop an overall theme or argument.

☐ The best way to see how dissertations work in your subject area is to look at some examples; you will probably find that your department holds copies of completed dissertations. Although these might not help you with your subject area, they will give you ideas about layout and structure, the expected length and format of introductions and conclusions, and the extent of the bibliography that is expected of you. If you do refer to the material in any of these dissertations, reference it as meticulously as you would any other source.

9 Exams and Revision

Many courses undertaken by mature students involve no exams and are assessed on coursework and practical field studies alone. However, even with no exams you might be called upon to revise and recall material, perhaps for a research panel exercise or in order to contribute convincingly to a conference discussion panel. Whatever the reason for having to take in and retain a bulk of information, your approach will be similar.

When it comes to revision you will probably be surprised at how much you have taken in already – most students are, if they give themselves the chance to reflect, and this is perhaps your first task. Assume that you will already know **50–60 per cent** of the information; in this way revision becomes a case of formalising and utilising what you already know, and trying to take in facts which have escaped you. If you have taken control of your learning in the ways suggested in this guide, you can be confident that you already know far more than you might expect, and the advice offered here will allow you to maximise on this benefit whilst absorbing additional information.

● Timing

There is no 'right' time to begin to plan your revision; it will depend entirely on the amount of information you need to absorb and the type of person you are. Some students, particularly if they have not faced exams for some years, much prefer to plan their revision very early, not least to reassure themselves that they are on top of the situation. Others prefer the last-minute push. Whichever system has worked well for you in the past is the one to adopt now, and if you cannot remember how you once coped with exams, then think about how you work generally, considering whether you tend naturally to be a last-minute person or a long-term planner.

The good news is that no time is 'too late' for revision planning. Even if you suspect that you have left your revision too late, you will still be able to allocate the time that is left by prioritising your revision tasks.

● Planning

As with any task, the planning for your revision will be as complex or simple as you choose to make it, but there are some key rules to follow:

1   **Include everything**: by including every possible revision task in your plan, you will avoid missing any areas and you will have the increased satisfaction of being able to tick many more tasks off your lists.

2   Decide how to **divide the revision tasks**. For most exams, students tend to work chronologically through their course and divide their subject area into building blocks as they have been presented to them. This works well, but you might also like to consider the task ahead of you. You will know how each exam is structured, and you will know the order of your exams, and so you might divide the material differently so as to reflect what is being asked of you, and when.

3   **Vary the tasks**. Revision tasks can become far too repetitive, and this is not a good way to take in information, so make sure that you plan to tackle different tasks in each session. You might spend some time reducing your notes to revision cards, some time reading through your existing tasks, some time (but not too much) reading through back-up material if you are unsure of an area, and some time making exam plans.

4   **Include easy tasks**. The point of having a revision timetable of some sort is not just to make sure that you can cover the material in the time available; it is also a way to make you feel good. It boosts your confidence each time you can tick a task off your list – so if, for example, you need to work through three lectures reducing them to manageable notes, and you know that this will take you no more than an hour, include it in your plan. An easy tick off the list, both satisfying and useful.

5   **Stop when it is done**. This is the most difficult challenge in revising. Students often lament the fact that their revision is mind-numbingly boring and that they don't seem to be getting anywhere. As soon as I hear this I know that they have got it wrong: either they are so distracted that they are not really absorbing what they are reading or – more likely – they know the information already and just keep reading through their notes or revision cards because they don't know when to stop. Test yourself frequently and make sure that you begin to use your material as you vary your tasks. You need never assume that you must retain 100 per cent of the facts, so make sure that, as soon as you feel reasonably confident, you move on to the next batch of material.

● Managing the material

Reams of notes are not going to help you much at this stage: they take ages to read through, include lots of irrelevant, incidental data, and are daunting in prospect. You will need to reduce all of the notes which you feel will be relevant to your exams onto revision cards. Use the 4" x 6" index cards which are available from any stationers and begin work. This is a really satisfying aspect of revising, because you are altering yourself from being a passive receptor of facts into an active user of those facts. On the cards, write down only the key facts which will help you to remember the whole set of information: avoid the temptation just to reproduce your notes onto cards. If you have time, as your revision progresses, you might return to a set of cards and reduce them even further. The pleasure in this task lies with the fact that you will be remembering the facts you need as you produce the cards, without any conscious effort on your part. Once the cards are ready, it is a simple task to read through each one, cover it up and test yourself on what you know. Towards exam time, you might also want to produce a few 'last-minute cards' – cards which show the absolutely most important facts to remember, or those facts which, however hard you try, you simply cannot make stay in your head for long (we all have some of these).

Your revision cards will also become a lasting record of what you have achieved. In years to come, you will be able to remind yourself with ease of the areas you have covered, and this can be useful when you come to choose another course, or you are asked to revisit an area. Just last week, I returned to some of my old revision cards to help guide a student through one aspect of an assessed essay; I am glad that I kept them to hand.

● Preparing

Students usually assume that doing well in exams is all about how much you know. It isn't – it is about how well you use what you know. Of course, you need to master most of the facts from your course of study, but in most subject areas it is far better to know 70 per cent of the facts and to use this knowledge wisely, with a mature and confident approach, than to know 90 per cent of the facts and yet have no idea how to apply them.

Indeed, facts are of very little value to you until you begin to use them, and that is why **exam planning** is so important. Using whichever planning method you prefer, produce as many plans as possible. Use past exam papers, or ask your tutor for some example questions, or simply make up likely questions yourself. This is active revising: each plan that you make will help you to grasp more fully the implications of the information you have absorbed, and the ways in which you might use it.

It is far more productive to make revision cards, master the facts and then make exam plans than it is to simply learn the facts and hope for the best; it is also better to stick to making plans, rather than writing out whole practice answers to possible questions. The reason for this is twofold: once you have an essay written out in your mind, it is far more difficult to write in a fresh, engaging and relevant way in the exam, and you run the risk of simply memorising whole sections of a prepared essay, which might work, until you lose your way and find yourself floundering; it is also far more difficult to adapt your material to answer a specific exam question if you already have a fully formed answer to another question in your memory. Even if you have a '**seen exam**', where you are given access to the exam paper in advance so that you can prepare, I would still advocate making a detailed exam plan rather than writing out your intended answer in full.

● In the exam

Just before you enter the exam room you will be looking at any last-minute cards you have produced. Once you are in the exam, take the following approach to exam answers, regardless of the subject matter of the exam.

Before you start to write:

- Divide your time between planning, writing and checking. In an hour-long exam, you would ideally spend 10 minutes planning, 45 minutes writing and 5 minutes checking.
- Read ALL the questions twice.
- Unburden your mind of all the 'rubbish' that will get in the way. This means writing down all of the facts that you put on your last-minute cards, so that you are not distracted by the worry of forgetting something. Also write down any material from your revision that you feel is putting up barriers to effective thinking.
- Read the questions again, confirming your choice.
- Remember how any mock exams that you gave yourself felt at this point: this will help to calm your nerves and focus your mind.
- Decide in advance whether to plan each answer at the beginning, or whether to plan each answer as you work through the paper.
- Decide in advance whether it is better for you to answer your 'strongest' question first or last.
- Make a six-point plan straight away (this takes two minutes).
- Read the question again.
- 'Flesh out' your six-point plan (this takes five minutes) using your preferred planning method. Does it still make sense? At this stage, include a note of quotes, dates, other texts that you might mention, your conclusion etc.
- Go back to the 'rubbish dump' of information you jotted down at the outset and see if anything from there needs to be included.

When you write:

- Work from your more detailed plan, but keep an eye on the time. Be prepared to abandon a point in the best way you can if you are running too far over on time, but allow the answer to flow naturally for as long as you can.
- If you have to leave a point, leave enough space so that you can direct the marker to work that you add later on.
- If you get desperate on time, you might need to direct the marker back to your plan so that s/he can see where you would have gone if there had been enough time.

If you wobble:

- Several peculiar things can happen to your brain in an exam:
    - You seem to be writing complete rubbish.
    - You lose the point of what you wanted to say.
    - You start to doubt that you have answered the right question.

    In fact, these are unlikely to be real problems, in that none of them will be a true reflection of the situation. What is really happening is that you are getting tired, or nerves are getting the better of you, or you have just had to go through too many exams in a short space of time. If this happens to you, stop writing for a few moments, take a breath and check back to your plan. This will ground you back in your main points and the whole process will become easier again.
- If, in the few seconds that you have taken a break, you decide that you really have gone off course, close the point you are making as soon as you can and move firmly on to your next point. This will probably appear seamless in your final script, and it will ensure that you keep on track.

Towards the end:

- Checking is always going to be important, but you have relatively little time to do this in an exam. If you have five minutes, you will have time to read your whole answer through for errors and inconsistency. This is going to be a better bet than simply continuing to write until the very end of the exam.
- If you are running out of time, and have only a couple of minutes to do some final checking, abandon the idea of reading through the entire script and instead look for typical weak points in each answer:
    - The opening: does it say what you mean?
    - The conclusion: is it strong enough?
    - Titles and dates: are they accurate?
    - Names: are they right?
    - Blanks and spaces: can you fill them in now?
    - Gaps left for more writing: do you have time now?
    - Three-quarters of the way through the answer: did you have a brainstorm? Does this portion of the answer actually make sense?

And when it is over:

Forget it. You know that you have worked hard for this exam. If you have a specific concern (did I get one particular fact right?) then you might check with a couple of your fellow students, but beyond this, post-mortems are rarely a good idea.

The following day, however, you might like to reflect upon your strengths and weaknesses whilst they are fresh in your mind. Make a note of what you intend to do differently in future exams. It is surprising how quickly the details of the experience fade from your mind, but notes made now will help you to focus your energy in future exams.

Contrary to popular belief, exams are an exciting time – you are finally getting the chance to show how well you have mastered your subject. You may never come to enjoy exams, but you can reach a point where your answers accurately reflect your knowledge base and ability, and this is always a satisfying place to be.

How to progress:

- [ ] Practise, practise, practise! From the earliest stages of your course you can begin to set yourself mock exam questions for each area of study, so that you can practise answering exam questions: this will usefully feed into the way in which you revise your material.

- [ ] Revision groups can be a good thing; they can also be a huge waste of time. If you are in an over-competitive group you can feel deflated each time you meet; if you are in an under-achieving group you will not be challenged sufficiently. Try out a revision group if your fellow students organise one – or organise it yourself if you would find it useful – but be prepared to revise alone, or with one study partner, if this suits you best.

- [ ] Online revision groups can be motivating. The same caution applies as to any revision group, but the advantage of an online chat room dedicated to revising a course – as long as you ignore the inevitable rumours and panics – is that you can access it at a time and stage in your revision that suits you.

10 Personal Development

Personal development is a unique process: as unique as you are. What happens to you as a student, how your experiences shape your sense of yourself, will be individual to you. How you might choose to reflect these changes in other areas of your life will also be up to you. However, what is undeniable is that you *will* change as a result of your study. To ignore this fact is not only to deny the benefits of studying, it is also to miss opportunities by keeping your eyes closed to change. There is a saying that 'Happiness comes through doors you did not realise were open'. The same is undoubtedly true of change, and that is the point of this section: to help you to recognise change and to take advantage of it.

Of course, you could resolutely refuse to change, and nobody could force you to do otherwise, but positive changes, the ones you can expect from being a student, are only truly daunting when we fail to understand why and how they are happening and how we can benefit from them.

When I was planning to begin a course of study as a mature student, the possibility of changes to me and my life were the last thing on my mind. I did not think about the effect a new qualification might have on my career, and I certainly did not consider how studying might change me. Indeed, I didn't especially want to be changed; I was happy enough as I was. Looking back, this seems naïve, but it is a common attitude amongst mature students. Inexorably, my life as a student changed me – not, perhaps, my fundamental values in life, but certainly my view of myself and my future. I had not expected to change career (then I became an academic); I had not hoped to become more visible (then I gave my first successful presentation); I did not aim to move beyond my first course (then I did a doctorate); and it never occurred to me to make new friends (and then they all arrived in my seminar group).

The point is that for most mature students, studying is a life-changing experience. This can be exciting at times, worrying at other times. It can make you feel more fulfilled; it can make you dissatisfied with your life. It can make you proud of your achievements; it can leave you frustrated that you did not start earlier. You will have some or all of these responses to study, and probably many more. By coming to terms with the inevitability of change, and analysing what is happening to you in a systematic way, you will be more able to see change as a positive aspect of your life as a mature student.

Most institutions run systems that are designed to help students to reflect upon their learning and the changes they are experiencing. This usually involves students filling out a **log or record** of their achievements and learning needs, sometimes alone, but more usually in discussion with a tutor. The idea of these systems is to encourage **reflective learning**. Most mature students work very well within this system. This is perhaps because they have already reflected on their learning needs before signing up for a course.

Most of us have learnt by rote at some stage in our lives. We learn, for example, the multiplication tables, and this is the perfect example of **one-step learning**. We learn the tables, usually by reciting them, and then, if asked, we can say without hesitation that seven times seven is forty-nine. We have achieved the primary learning task. What is missing, if no reflective learning is included in the system, is the bigger picture. We might not know that seven is a prime number, we might not be able to estimate roughly the value of seven times seven, we might not be able to apply our rote learning to anything else. So whilst we have learned something, and this certainly has its uses, we have learned far less than we might have done.

At a higher level of learning, the ideal is to work towards **REAL learning**, that is, **Reflective, Effective, Active Learning**. The idea is that you will take a single learning experience, and reflect upon it so that you can make it effective (usually by applying the experience to another challenge) and then take an active role in maximising the benefits of the experience (such as using it as a springboard to the next challenge you have set yourself).

● REAL learning

The example of a lecture will demonstrate this well:

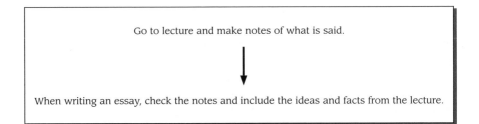

This is typical one-step learning. Although the student may also check out some reference books for the essay, or may record laboratory work, or interviews, essentially the process is one step. It is time-consuming, lacks connectivity and tends to produce disappointing results.

A REAL approach to this lecture would be quite different. The first stage is the same as for the one-step learning student, as both will attend the same lecture.

Attending the lecture

Task:

Took notes in the lecture, having thought beforehand about why I was there and what I needed to know for my essay and my subject area generally.

Reflective result:

Know more about the subject area.
Developed my listening skills.
Developed my note-taking skills.

Effective result:

I need to improve my IT skills but don't have time at the moment to attend a course – could lectures help?

Active result:

Use my laptop in the next couple of lectures to see if I can practise touch-typing whilst I am in there.

The two types of student have now parted company. Whilst the one-step student will file the lecture notes away until writing the essay, the REAL learner will continue, reworking the lecture notes.

Reworking the lecture notes

Task:

Go through the notes, make a note of any original ideas offered in the lecture, note the secondary reading that was suggested, mark up those areas where I might disagree with the current debate so that I can look at them more closely.

Reflective result:

There are some ideas here that I could apply to my dissertation. Even though it is covering a different subject area, the general ideas from this lecture could be discussed in it. I know where I need to go for the reading for my essay.
There are a couple of points I need to work on before I plan the essay – the seminar should help me with these.

Effective result:

I don't know enough about one of the references given in the lecture – check it out before I use it.

Active result:

Targeted secondary reading.
Prepare questions for next seminar to save me some background reading time.

Unlike many one-step learners, the reflective learner will now plan the essay. In this case, reflection on the task does not lead to any effective or active results, so there is no chain of action as a result of the planning.

Planning the essay

> **Task:**
>
> Plan the essay once the secondary reading has been done and after the seminar where we discussed the areas I was unsure about and confirmed that it was fine for me to disagree with one aspect of the critical debate.

> **Reflective result:**
>
> I am happy with my essay-planning skills – they are one of my strengths.

Now both students will write the essay. Even at this stage, the REAL learner will be adding to the task to accrue more benefits.

Writing the essay

> **Task:**
>
> Write the essay, following the plan I made and using all of my secondary material.

> **Reflective result:**
>
> I need to improve my essay-writing skills.

Effective result:

I structure my essays well and am clear on what I want to say. What I need is help with my grammar and punctuation.

Active result:

Book onto a study skills class on grammar and punctuation.

It is not difficult to work out which of the two students will produce the better essay, but the point of REAL learning is greater than this: the REAL learner has made the whole learning experience more productive.

The one-step learner might be expected to have produced the essay more quickly, even if it is of a lesser quality. In practice, though, this student will:

- have wandered around the library or resource centre for a couple of hours, with no clear idea of what to read, then wasted more time making notes on books which might or might not be helpful;
- have added a set of untouched lecture notes to the pile of notes which he or she will have to go through at revision time – a mammoth task;
- be unsure about where help might be needed in essay writing, so will one day attend several general essay-writing workshops, wasting time if only one, targeted session is really needed;
- feel less confident about the looming dissertation, because the clues in the lecture have been missed;
- have become demotivated about going to lectures, having missed much of the value of this one;
- feel an occasional sense of panic that things are running out of control, but have no clear idea of how to address the problem.

The REAL learner will have worked harder at the process, but will actually have saved time by:

- planning to use a laptop in the next few lectures for improved IT skills, rather than going on an IT course;

COOKLANDS COLLEGE LIBRARY
WEYBRIDGE, SURREY KT13 8TT

Task: (what am I doing?)

Reflective result: (what have I learnt from this?)

Effective result: (where do I need to develop?)

Active result: (what should I do to make this happen?)

Table 9

© Lucinda Becker (2009), *The Mature Student's Handbook*,
Palgrave Macmillan Ltd

- only reading those secondary texts which were relevant to this essay;
- using the seminar following the lecture to get some answers, thus saving hours in the library;
- already having some dissertation ideas, which will save time in the future;
- reworking the lecture notes not just for this essay, but ready for revision, which will save huge amounts of time later;
- having booked onto just one, targeted study skills session on grammar;
- feeling more confident about the skills that are in place, and the process of learning, so time is not wasted worrying vaguely about it all, or working on study areas where there is no need to spend the time.

Table 9 gives you the chance to put the theory into practice for the next few learning experiences you have. These might include attending a lecture, a class or a seminar, or carrying out experimental work, or working through a reading list. Whatever the task, there will be a REAL opportunity within it.

Any personal development system within an educational institution is simply intended to support this REAL learning process. If you can achieve this level of reflective learning for a series of single tasks, it is only a small step to being able to see your entire course in this way. Once you begin to do this, you can target your energy where it will be of most value, you can work with your tutor to get the help that you need, and you can begin to plan future courses and areas of study in an effective way. REAL learning moves studying into a new dimension: it makes it a far more sophisticated and rewarding experience.

How to progress:

☐ This is one aspect of your studying in which you can easily, and usefully, involve your fellow students. Ask them what they have noticed about how you talk about your course, how you approach your study, how you seem to feel about what you are doing and how it is working for you. Although they might not all know exactly what your course involves, you might be surprised at how astute their appraisal of your development is.

☐ At the outset of your course, try writing a 'wish list' of things which you hope will change for you as a result of studying, then firmly hide it away until the mid-point on your course. Then, take a look and see not only how near you have come to achieving those 'wish list' goals, but also, perhaps, how your aspirations have altered as a result of your student experience.

11 Organising Your Time

Timing can be a particular challenge for mature students. If you are on a full-time course, it can feel as if you have too much unstructured time to work with; on a part-time course (especially if you also have a job and/or a family) you can feel squeezed on time from every direction; if you are on a distance learning course it can be difficult to judge whether you are devoting too much, or too little, time to your studies.

The chart in Checklist 6 shows extracts from recent interviews with mature students. Tick any boxes that reflect how you feel. Although this chart may seem to cover quite a range of issues, in fact each of these can be traced back to problems with timing. If you have ticked more than two boxes, you probably need to work out a plan which helps you to use your time more effectively. Some people are not natural planners, but this need not get in the way of benefiting from a **personalised timetable**: you can make it as loose or rigid as you need it to be.

● Personalised timetable

You will already have a timetable in place for your studies, even if it is no more than a list of deadlines to meet. With a personalised timetable you will be able to see, at a glance, how all of the different areas of your study, and your life, fit together.

You will make your own choices about how complicated your personalised timetable needs to be, and which columns you need to include, but the example in Table 10 will give you an idea of how it works. This example timetable gives an outline: yours is likely to be far more detailed. It is worth thinking about how each of these columns works.

Timetabled study
This column should run itself – it includes all of the timetabled events on your course. It is included so that you never miss anything, but also so that you know in advance which are going to be your busiest timetabled weeks, so that you can adjust the other columns accordingly.

Assessed work
Once you have completed each week's tasks, you can take a break, knowing that you are keeping up with your commitments. If you are doing group work, such as a group presentation, you will be able to arrange rehearsals on those weeks when it is most

CHECKLIST 6

	✔
I have good and bad days. Sometimes I feel completely on top of things; other days, it all seems a bit of a mess.	
I struggle to stay motivated, even though I know this is a course that interests me.	
I hate the deadlines: they always seem to catch me unawares, even though I know I am working hard.	
I look around and think that everyone is getting on better than me, but I cannot see what they are doing differently.	
I mostly find my course interesting, but I never seem to get the time to enjoy it properly.	
The pressure never seems to lift; I am always racing from one thing to the next, always feeling that I am not quite making it.	
There is so much that I want to do, but there never seems to be enough time to do it.	
I often feel that I am neglecting something, either my job, or my studies, or my family.	
I often wake up early worrying about the amount I have to do, so then I get up and work on something.	
I struggle to complete anything. I start one thing, and then realise another thing is more important, so I have to move on to that.	
I thought there would be more to studying than this: there is so much more I would like to do, but there is no time.	

convenient for you, rather than feeling pressurised by your other commitments when you want to focus on that one task.

Reading

Use your personalised timetable to tame your reading lists: work out what you really need to read, and what you can realistically expect to get through, then include it in your timetable so that you will have the satisfaction of being able to tick it off as you go – and relax about the whole process.

© Lucinda Becker (2009), *The Mature Student's Handbook*, Palgrave Macmillan Ltd

Wish list

This is the most creative column in the timetable. It is where you put all those things that you would really love to do if only you could find the time. Just entering these things on your timetable will make you feel more motivated. Using this column means that you will not waste time wondering what to do next, or starting a task which then gets left midway through. You will not always be able to tick off every item in this column, but you will know that it is not a disaster if this happens: usually, an item can be re-entered later in the timetable if you don't get around to it in the week you first planned to do it.

	Timetabled study	Assessed work	Reading	Wish list	Life outside study
Week One	Start of Wed 10 a.m. lectures. Seminar on advanced statistics.	Plan week 4 essay.	Read guest speaker's advanced material.	Sort last term's practicals file.	Check with Beth on vacation work.
Week Two	Guest speaker on standard deviation. No seminar.	Finish preparing for seminar presentation and practise it in group. Check essay plan with tutor.	Background reading for essay.	Mature students' group social – get details.	Jo's birthday.
Week Three	Late lecture on psycho- metrics. My seminar.	Give seminar presentation.	Read Jenkin's article on probability – do the practical prep sheet?	Go to study skills dept revision session.	Book holiday.
Week Four	Meeting with personal tutor – arrange for morning session. Seminar on probability.	Write essay.		Tidy up lecture notes for this month and file. Time to join maths group internet forum?	Work with Jeff on setting up his internet business.

Table 10

Life outside study

We tend to run most of our lives on autopilot, dashing from one task to the next in the hope of scooping up and doing all of the things that need to be done. The ability to multi-task, so lacking in many younger students, is usually very well developed in mature students. This is, of course, to your advantage, but it does mean that, with the pressure of study, you might be working hard and yet still feel that there are tasks looming all around you. By completing this column you will be prioritising the essential tasks, and also reminding yourself that, however demanding your course, you do have a life outside it.

● Sharing your timetable

A personalised timetable is an excellent **communication tool**, so spread it around. Share it with your tutor so that your plans are clear and you can receive advice on how to maximise your study time; show it to your family so that they too have some sense of when you are likely to be most busy (and can remind you of any family commitments to be added); put it up somewhere prominent so that you can glance at a snapshot of where you are and where you are going, whenever you like.

● Making time

This can seem like a dream come true – to find that you have more hours in the week to study – but actually it is relatively simple to achieve. Ironically, to do this will take up some of your time at the outset, but it will pay dividends later. For one week, make a note at the end of the day of roughly how you spent each hour (this is the time-consuming bit); then, at the end of the week, work out where and how you could effectively **'double up' on your time**. Examples of this would include reworking your lecture notes on a regular train journey, reading whenever you find yourself regularly waiting in your car for something, working through your reading lists in the last, least productive half hour in the library. Once you become an expert at this doubling up, you will find that you are checking your recall of radio programmes, to develop your memory; that you can rework notes whilst you watch television; that you set aside ten minutes of a regular lunch date with a fellow student for you both to recap on the salient points of that morning's lecture or seminar.

We all have 'dead time' in our lives, it's part of how we relax, but analysing this time in your life is likely to throw up regular possibilities for doubling up to study along with your other activities – and so 'extra time' magically appears.

● Taking control

This whole process is about taking control: of your time, your tasks, your life. The blank timetable provided in Table 11 gives you the chance to begin working in this system.

	Timetabled study	Assessed work	Reading	Wish list	Life outside study
Week One					
Week Two					
Week Three					
Week Four					

Table 11

© Lucinda Becker (2009), *The Mature Student's Handbook*,
Palgrave Macmillan Ltd

Once you have used this for four weeks you will be ready to produce your own, more detailed and personalised timetable.

How to progress:

☐ You are, and will remain, the best judge of how well you are using your time, but input from others can help in some ways. If you know that some of your fellow students are also using personalised timetables, comparing theirs to yours might give you some useful ideas as to how yours might develop.

☐ It is easy to be unrealistic about your timetable, which leaves you feeling constantly under pressure because you seem always to be altering it to compensate for the work you have not been able to complete in your allotted time span. If this keeps happening to you, don't assume that you are not working hard enough; instead, show your tutor your timetable and work together to make it more achievable.

☐ Once you have tried out a personalised timetable in the chart above, think about how you might change, or add to, the column headings to suit your needs.

12 Sorting Out Your Money

It perhaps goes without saying that studying can be expensive, but, for mature students, there might also be hidden costs. If you are reducing your regular salary to study part time, or stopping paid work altogether, it can be difficult to gauge the **long-term impact** of such a move at the outset. If you hope to protect your income by undertaking a distance learning course, intending to work in the evenings or at weekends, it can come as a surprise to realise that you might need some extra time off work when it comes to assignments or placements.

Beyond this, the financial world of a mature student can seem deceptively simple. You might be used to budgeting, but how do you budget accurately for a course when you have no idea of exactly how many books you will have to buy; cannot tell from one term to the next how many days a week you will have to attend your place of learning; do not know in advance how many extras (such as lab costs, field trips, study placements etc.) might be involved?

Despite this, you should be able to produce at least a **preliminary budget**, and you will be given notice of many of the extra costs at least a little in advance. You may have been planning your course for some time, and so have some contingency money in place, or you might be able to work in the evenings or vacations to top up your income. The answer to many financial problems is flexibility – being prepared to budget and re-budget as necessary, and facing up to financial problems as early as you can.

The first thing to consider, even before you begin your course, is whether you can find any financial support for the course itself. Some institutions offer **studentships**, **bursaries** and **scholarships**, for example, whilst some educational charities are dedicated to helping students; there are funding bodies out there of which you may never have heard. The first place to turn for help is to the institution itself. As soon as you register an interest in a course, you will be able to get advice on funding. The best place to start is the Careers Service of your institution, as the advisers there should be able to help you directly, or point you in the direction of Student Services, who may have details of local educational charities.

It is worth remembering that many **employers** will help pay towards the costs of a course, even if the qualification is not directly relevant to the work that you are doing. For many mature students their entire course is funded by their employer; for others the situation is less clear. I have been amazed over the years at how many mature students have had their courses paid for by employers, who want to be seen as investors in people, and view this type of support as part of their remit – it is one of the huge potential advantages of being a mature student. Don't assume that your employer won't help until you have asked – it may even be worth your while to change your plans (doing a part-time rather than a full-time course so that you can also work part-time, for example) in order to get the help. At the very least it will mean that your employer is aware of your situation when you later come to ask for extra leave as a deadline approaches.

● Reducing your running costs whilst you study

Each mature student will be working in different circumstances, and each course has a different set of requirements, so what is offered here in Checklist 7 is a range of suggestions that might help you to balance your budget. You could tick each box as you put the suggestions into place, and there are blank spaces for you to fill in as your course progresses. Ask your study colleagues what they are doing to save money, or make money, and fill in the spaces to motivate you to follow the advice that makes sense for you and your circumstances.

● Earning money

There are two reasons why you might be thinking about earning some cash whilst you study: either it was always part of your plan (maybe you are studying part time and earning as well) or you have run out of money and need to earn some to balance your budget. In either case, you will want to think about the best way to go about this. If you are working part time already, **review your options** from time to time to make sure that you are making the most of your earning potential; if you need to earn some extra cash you will want to make it worth your while. Checklist 8 will help you to do this.

● Sorting out financial problems

It is easy enough with hindsight to see that facing up to financial problems as they are looming on the horizon is a better idea than trying to solve them once you are engulfed: it is, of course, far more difficult when you are the one facing the problems. In general, mature students have the life experience and financial acumen to reduce their money problems and to deal with them effectively, but that does not mean that it will never happen to you.

With this thought in mind, as soon as you start to worry that you do not have enough money, sit down and make a budget. **Include everything and be realistic** – this is not the time to work out what you would like to happen; you need to be clear about what you really spend. Once you have produced a budget, leave it be for a day or so, to give you the chance to look at it anew and make sure that you have left nothing out. Ideally, share it with a friend who can remind you of anything that you have forgotten.

CHECKLIST 7

	✔
Don't buy any books until you have checked that you really need them – borrow them from the library first.	
If you have to buy books, check out the noticeboards or departmental newsletter and the internet for cheap, second-hand copies.	
Try to avoid using expensive eating places on campus. This sounds obvious, but frothy, expensive cappuccinos can be very tempting; just two cups a day could cost you £300 for the term.	
Time is money: even on a full-time course you can often arrange your on-campus activities so that you reduce the number of days you have to attend, thus freeing up more of your private study time and reducing your travelling costs.	
Share lifts where you can, and remember that students of all ages can get student discount cards for all sorts of things, including travel. An international student card might also give you cheaper flights, so you might save in other ways, too.	
If you are distance learner, try to be as disciplined as you can about arranging your studying into blocks of time, as this will free up time in which you could earn money.	
If you are required to undertake an expensive field trip or study outing, find out if your institution can offer any help with the costs, and try to reduce the cost as much as you can at the outset.	
Don't join any student group or society unless you know that you will really benefit from it and have time to get involved. Your membership fee is only worth it if you are an active member of the group.	
If you are working on a group project, having some virtual meetings over the internet can help to reduce your travel costs and move things on even when you are working from home.	

Now you need to work out a **financial strategy**, and this will come in two parts: dealing with your debt and covering your running costs. Dealing with your debt needs to be a long-term plan, working out the options available to you to make it cheaper and less immediately stressful. **Consolidating your debt** might be a good idea, but only if you can make it cheaper – which means avoiding any company which offers to make life easier but which is not a reputable firm. If you have always assumed that there is no funding available to you, this would be the time to check: there are educational grants

© Lucinda Becker (2009), *The Mature Student's Handbook*, Palgrave Macmillan Ltd

CHECKLIST 8

	✔
Go through your budget again and make it as realistic as you can, especially if you are getting into difficulty. It is better to know the true scale of the problem and earn enough money, rather than make changes in your study pattern and then still find that you need to earn more money and, perhaps, be forced to take another job.	
Decide in advance which portions of time would be best for you to use to earn money: daytime, evenings, weekends, vacations. This is going to be especially important if you are aiming to work throughout most of your course.	
Work out other factors which might be important to you, such as flexi-time, the option of more, or fewer, hours in the future, location and childcare.	
All of this has been done before you even begin to think about a job title. When you get to this stage, don't assume that you just need to accept any job that is offered to you. One of the advantages of being a mature student is that you will probably have the experience to get a better-paid job rather than a 'typical' student job. Work out what skills you are offering.	
Check out the best-paying jobs in your area: call centre jobs and office jobs often pay better than restaurant or bar jobs, for example. Working in a job share in a higher-level job rather than one offered part-time can increase your earnings. Decide if you are prepared to travel to earn more money, if this is likely to be a factor.	
Ask your fellow students and/or your tutors about the local job market – inside information can make a big difference to your job search.	
If you are on a campus-based course, don't overlook the possibility of working on your campus. This might offer you a job with no travel costs, flexible hours and good pay. Ask at the Careers Service of your institution, and check the student website or jobs newsletter regularly.	
Don't assume that, just because you need the cash, you shouldn't look at the possibility of a job that is in some way related to your studying. If you get a job which has some bearing on your area of study, you are likely to find it more interesting and you can use your study to promote yourself at interview.	
If you can't find a job which interests you, or which pays well enough, you might think about a job which offers you time to study whilst you earn. Working a night shift in a petrol station, for example, might not sound like the most exciting job in the world, and the pay may not be fantastic, but you will have plenty of free time to read and plan essays and so on whilst you earn.	

© Lucinda Becker (2009), *The Mature Student's Handbook*, Palgrave Macmillan Ltd

and loans, cheap overdrafts for students, career development loans, and your Student Services Office (usually part of your Students' Union) should know about all of these options.

Most students would opt at this stage to reduce their outgoings and earn some money to cover their running costs, even if they had not planned to do so at the outset of their course. This might work for you – and the charts above will help you to work through this option – but it might be that you are simply not in a position to take on paid work at this stage in your course. If this is the case for you, you might need to look at the option of increasing your debt temporarily, but you might also want to consider your institution's **Student Hardship Fund**. These funds are in place at most institutions; they are usually administered by the Student Services Office and they can be a lifesaver. Contact your Student Union in the first instance (or check the institution's website – the forms to fill out are often lodged online), but be prepared to have to fill in forms and make a case for yourself. You will have to be able to show either that your circumstances have unexpectedly changed, such as losing your job, and that you need help until you can work out a solution, or that your studying requirements are such that you cannot earn money for a time, but that the problem is temporary, that you have a solution in place for the future. If you can do this, a hardship fund can be a great way to ease your financial burden.

There might also be help available through the government-funded **Access to Learning Fund**: again, your Student Services or Careers Service will be able to offer you support in applying for these funds.

Perhaps the best financial advice any mature student can be offered is **not to suffer alone**. Get help as early as you can, face your problems before they overwhelm you, and make sure that you research thoroughly every possible source of help.

How to progress:

☐ In the first (and second, and third) instance, avoid approaching anyone for help who actually wants to make huge amounts of money from you: that is, credit card companies, 'pay off all your debts in one go' adverts and those who offer expensive unsecured loans. Go instead to those you can trust first, to get an impartial overview of your finances, and then approach low-interest credit providers, but only if borrowing money is the best option.

☐ Your welfare office (usually part of your Students' Union) is a good place to visit, not just for help in raising finance, but also for practical, knowledgeable advice.

☐ Your bank advisers or bank manager will want to lend you money, but they will also want to keep your long-term custom, so they might also be worth approaching for some advice about how you can best budget, and what, if any, low-interest loans or student overdrafts might be available to you.

13 Help and Support

When you were choosing your course, you will have looked at the details of the studying involved and the qualification you will get at the end. You are less likely to have chosen a particular place to study because of the wider support it offers you, but this is an important part of what you are being offered by your institution.

Like many mature students, I did not expect to find much support for my studying within my institution. I am reasonably self-reliant and presumed that I would sort out any problems that arose by myself, or with the help of family and friends. This worked, to a point, but I wasted far too much time and energy worrying about problems that I could have fixed relatively easily if I had known where to go, and going 'the long way around' rather than taking the easiest route. The advice being offered in this chapter is based upon all of the things I learnt only after I completed my studying; I was amazed to find out, too late, just how much help was on offer.

The reason it is worth considering what help is available is twofold: it will allow you to take advantage of all that is on offer, and it means that you know straight away where to go if you need help. Each institution will vary a little, but you can expect that your place of study is likely to be structured in the way shown in Figure 12. At different stages in your course you will tap into the help offered from different quarters: the outlines offered here will help you to go to the right place at the right time.

⬤ For your help

Medical centre: if you are studying on a lengthy course, you might be offered the services of a medical centre on or near your campus. This is convenient; consider before you register whether it is worth transferring your records to a centre away from your home for the duration of your course, and note that there is sometimes an administration fee charged for the service. Emergency appointments are usually available even if you have not registered at the outset.

Counselling service: you might assume that you will never need this service, but it is worth checking out what it offers. Generally, counselling services at educational institutions do not expect to deal only with cases of mental illness; they often provide more general help to students, such as how to deal with revision stress, or coping with exams, or handling your nerves in presentations. It is a good idea to have a look at their website or go along to one of their events just to see what is available.

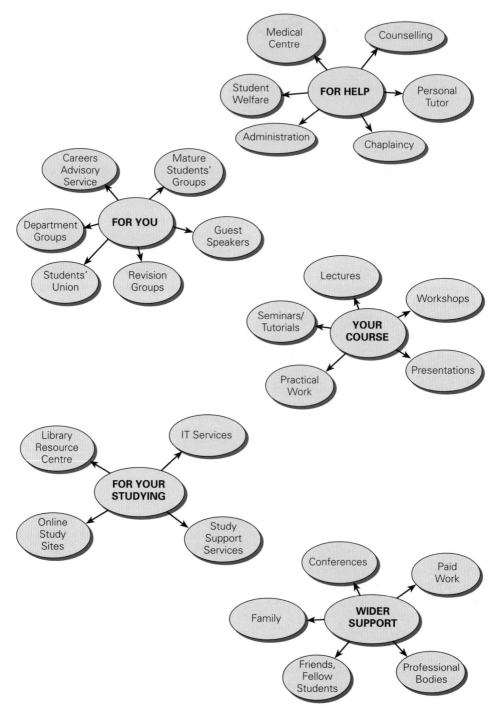

Figure 12

Administration: the secretaries and administrators in your department are the best place to start if you have practical problems or are confused about any of the forms you have to fill in. They deal with many students each day, and are used to being asked these questions: they often know more than the academics about the practicalities of a course. Small, niggling problems can sometimes become very distracting, so go to them sooner rather than later if a problem arises.

Personal tutor: this is a crucial relationship. If your institution runs a personal tutor system, you will meet with your tutor regularly to discuss your progress. You can make the most of the relationship by taking some control: share your personalised timetable with your tutor, and prepare for your meetings in advance. Remember that your personal tutor is usually the person who will give you a reference in the future, so it is a relationship worth cultivating.

Chaplaincy: your institution might or might not have an official chaplaincy service (most do), but there will be groups within the institution representing most religions, and they will hold regular events for support and worship, as well as counselling.

Student Services: this will be a major aspect of your Students' Union as well as other support departments. Welfare services are not always well advertised, and might be hidden away in back offices, but it is worth checking out the Student Union website and the general institution website. Support groups will offer help with housing, money, study skills, stress, practical problems and the representation of students. Mature students' groups often come under this support system. You might be surprised at the range of help that is on offer, for free and without even having to make an appointment.

● For you

Careers Advisory Service: students tend to approach the Careers Advisory Service (CAS) only when they are coming to the end of their course, so that they can get help in finding a job. It is far better to go along earlier than that. Mature students can find this service particularly useful – you might already have a career and so might need help in working out how your new qualification, and the skills you have gained, might impact upon your next career move. Your CAS will offer you mock interviews, psychometric tests, help with your CV and application forms, as well as both helping with career development and looking into the possibility of moving on to a further course of study. Although your CAS will help with long-term career goals, it is also a useful source of information about short-term jobs whilst you study, or for helping you with contacts if you need to organise a work placement during your course.

Mature students' groups: these are usually run by the Students' Union, and are dedicated to the needs of mature students. Students sometimes shy away from such groups, reluctant to be 'labelled' as mature, rather than just a student; nevertheless they do offer you the chance to network with other students who might face similar challenges to your own. They can be a useful place to get practical support, such as arranging lift shares, or finding fellow mature students on your course who can share their lecture notes with you if you have to miss a lecture. These groups usually run a website, so you will be able to see what they offer before you commit to joining.

Department groups: these groups are usually well advertised, and might be arranged for your whole department, or just for your course. They are sometimes run by a student society within your department, or by your lecturers, and tend to cover areas such as preparing for presentations, revision sessions, essay writing practice and extended discussions on topic areas. These are informal groups, encouraging discussion rather than being heavily structured, and can offer valuable support and guidance in key areas. If this type of group does not exist already in your department, or for your course, you might think of getting together with a couple of other students and starting one. They usually meet over lunchtime, or in the evenings, sometimes with visiting tutors who come along to share their expertise and experience. Groups like this can become an unexpected source of support in other areas, such as sharing lifts, or childcare, or reading groups.

Students' Union: the activities of Students' Unions differ from place to place, and most students know them for their social benefits: gigs and other social events on campus. Their remit is far wider than this, of course. As well as the Student Services already mentioned, they also run clubs and societies. Students think straight away of sporting clubs, but they actually run a huge number of clubs, covering many interests; just make sure that you will have the time and energy to get involved before you pay to join a club. The Students' Union building is often a centre for activities, and spending time there can help make you feel part of the life of a student; it offers a cheap and accessible social life on campus.

Guest speakers: educational institutions frequently invite guest speakers to give talks, and most of these events are open to all students and staff. The problem sometimes is finding out about them: ask your course secretary where they are advertised (usually a general website). Sometimes you will see instantly the relevance of attending these events: if you are studying history, talks in literature, philosophy or classical studies might all be of direct use to you in your study. On the other hand, if you are studying nursing, you might wonder why you should want to go to a talk entitled 'The Role of the Church in Modern Britain'. It is about how you feel as a student. Taking an hour off from your studying to attend a talk of general interest will give you a break from just focusing on your subject, and can make you feel that you are really benefiting from education in its widest form. These talks tend not to be easily available elsewhere, so it makes sense to take advantage of them whilst you are studying.

Revision groups: the potential benefit of these groups is easy to see, but finding them can be less easy. Some central support groups (Student Services, Counselling, Study Skills) will offer sessions in revision, but so too do student groups, and individual departments, and course leaders. It is the type of group you could easily set up for yourself. If you know that you will have problems as you approach exam time, these groups can be of benefit, but a note of caution is needed. Revision groups can become a waste of your time. Some students find that they increase the pressure on them; some feel that they are too competitive and just make them feel worse; some find them too prescriptive, seeming to suggest that there is only one 'right' way to deal with exams. Think carefully about how much a revision group can help you before you join one.

● For your studying

IT services: it is easy to assume that all the IT services department will offer you is an email account whilst you are studying, but in fact there is usually much more than this on offer, including drop-in sessions to help you make the most of new software, workshops to help you develop your IT skills and often a helpdesk where you can get immediate support. As the services on offer are not always well publicised, it is a good idea to go along to the department, or look at their website, even before your course begins, so that you can plan how best to use them. In this way, you might get free training in a variety of IT areas, which will boost your CV and aid your studying.

Study support: there may be times when you want to attend sessions run by your study support service to help you with aspects of your studying, such as planning essays, writing reports or giving presentations. Study support is usually not offered for each department, but for your institution as a whole, and the sessions will be fully booked as exam time approaches. If you do not have the time to attend sessions, or you do not feel that you need that level of support, it is still worth finding out about the supporting material that is offered: leaflets, web-based self-directed learning and drop-in sessions might all be available. Look into this early, so you know what is available before you need it.

Online study: online study sites (or web-based learning platforms, as they are sometimes called) are likely to be provided by your course leaders. If you are a distance learner, they will form the bulk of your study experience. You will be offered help on how to use these sites, and it is worth getting to grips with them as, increasingly, all of the information for courses is being lodged on such sites. It can be confusing if you are expecting to get reading lists, lecture timetables and seminar details on handouts or notices, only to find that you have to log on to a study site to find them. Even if you are still offered some information in hard copy, course websites and learning platforms will offer you a far richer range of material. As with any system, mistakes can happen, so if you think you should be registered on a site (either for a specific course or a more general study site) and you cannot find it, tell your course tutor straight away. Online study sites not created by your institution can be a valuable asset, but they are also a minefield: some will be very useful, some will be useless, some will encourage you to pay for essays, some might lead you into plagiarism (using someone else's words without acknowledging it) almost without you realising it. Some sites seem to be authoritative, yet are actually written by non-experts. If you want to use *any* website which has not been directly recommended by a tutor, make sure that you *always* check in advance whether it is a recommended site.

Library/resource centre: a tour of the main library or resource centre at your institution is likely to be part of your induction to study, but you might also consider access to other, less obvious resources. Departments sometimes have smaller departmental libraries, or study skills centres, and these are often underused. Once you find them you might have the advantage of being able to get hold of books and other resource materials more easily, and be able to keep them for longer than books that are much in demand from your main library or resource centre.

● Wider support

Conferences: students often overlook conferences as a source of support. However long or short your course, attending a conference is a good idea. Conferences will be held by academics in your field, and also, perhaps, by professional bodies in your area of work or study. As well as being of interest to you as you study, they are great places to meet others working in your subject area. They are useful for networking, both for your long-term career plans and for more immediate help in your studying. Speaking at a conference can seem daunting, but it is worth considering, as you will get plenty of feedback to help you move forward in your studying, and your expenses for the conference might be reimbursed. If you don't have the time or the money to attend a conference, it is still worth contacting the conference organisers, as the details of the conference (including all of the papers that were given) will usually be lodged on a website or published in a journal after the event. If you are not sure which conferences are being planned in your area, ask your tutor for help, so that you can be added to a conference's mailing list, or register with a conference alert website.

Work: although you might be working just to earn some money, try not to overlook the other potential advantages of the situation. Your employer might pay towards some of your course costs, even if you have already begun the course. At the least you might be offered practical support such as extra leave or flexible hours to help you with your studying. One way you can gain leverage for support is to offer the payback of sharing your new knowledge with your colleagues. Lunchtime talks (often called 'toolbox talks') to your colleagues need not be an onerous task, but they offer your employer a real incentive to support you.

Professional bodies: mature students who are studying in order to make a career move (or are aiming to progress in their chosen career) often assume that they should wait until they qualify before joining a professional body. This overlooks the advantages of 'student rate' membership (sometimes called 'associate membership') of a body, which is usually relatively cheap, can last for a year or so after you qualify and still gives you the benefits of membership, such as members' access to their website, reduced subscription to their professional journal, and lower conference costs. Apart from the obvious advantage of knowing about career development in your chosen area, professional bodies are a showcase for cutting-edge research (often some time before it is published anywhere else) and will give you access to details of other courses of study in your area, all of which could help in your planning for the future.

Friends and fellow students: this is an obvious area of support, but it needs some thought. Your friends outside your course may have very little idea of what you are actually doing: they will want to help but will need you to tell them how best to do this. Fellow students will have many of the same pressures and concerns as you, but if they are younger they may not always appreciate the particular challenges you face (and, equally, they will not always appreciate the advantages you have as a mature student). You might be apprehensive at first about how well you will get along with younger students, but in my experience this is rarely a problem: once in a seminar room, all students work together regardless of age. Although you will probably want to benefit from friendships with fellow students, you might need to be clear about when you will be available, so as to be sure that other students know how you are juggling your other commitments and your study time. In practice, this will not be a hurdle to friendships: as long as you are clear about your availability, your fellow students will be happy to work around your needs, as you will work around theirs.

Family: in some ways your family will offer similar support and offer the same challenges as your friendships, except of course that they have a vested interest in your succeeding, and they might well expect to be involved in your future planning. Try not to assume that, just because they are your family, they will know what is going on at all times; they may have only the sketchiest idea of what you actually do all day. Whilst there is little point in boring them with every detail of your course, it is a good idea to share your personalised timetable with them, so that they know when you will be most busy and, more importantly, when you might have some spare time. Finances will loom large from the outset, and any budget you produce for yourself is also worth sharing, especially if it is rather tentative, and you might need more money in the future. The same principle applies to your future plans. If your family is expecting you to complete a nine-month course, and you decide to go on to do a more advanced course, lasting a further two years, this is news best shared at the earliest planning stages, rather than presenting it as a surprise in the last few weeks of your course. Sharing your timetable, finances and future planning with your family helps you: involving them beyond that might not. Some mature students bring family members along to social events, or to conferences or guest talks. They have the best of intentions, of course – that of trying to involve their family in their studying – but this seems often to backfire, as there can be advantages to keeping your study and your home life separate. This will vary from person to person, but there is no need to feel guilty if you would rather be a student, by yourself, for some of the time.

How to progress:

☐ Whatever help and advice system you use, the support you are offered will always begin with your needs. Although you won't want to spend your time expecting things to go wrong, a monthly check on how things are going, where you jot down notes about areas of concern or success, can be reassuring; it can also help you spot problems as soon as they arise.

14 Embracing Change

● The new you

The REAL approach to your studying, as outlined in the Personal Development chapter of this guide, will help you to track the academic changes in your life: you now need to **maximise** upon all of the changes that are taking place.

Mature students can be resistant to the idea of change in themselves, and this is understandable. Whilst younger students expect a course of study to be part of the 'growing-up process', mature students who are perfectly happy with themselves and their lives might find change far less welcome, especially if they have already compartmentalised their studying along the lines of 'this is just for me, nothing to do with the rest of my life', or 'I just need this qualification for my career, I have no time to think of anything else'.

Of course, changes in you and the way you look at yourself and life in general will not be stopped by any preconceptions you have, and it makes sense to **run a check** on how you are developing as a person and a student every two or three months. There are several reasons for this:

1   It helps you to recognise the progress you are making, both in your specific course and as a learner generally.
2   Your recognition of change will feed into your attitude towards the next set of challenges, making it more likely that you will face them with confidence.
3   It allows you to take stock of other areas of your life, so you will be well placed to transfer new skills and attitudes to your career or your recreational life.
4   It guides you towards the future, helping you to plan the next stages of your career, or consider the possibility of a further course of study.

Outlined in Checklist 9 are areas of your development that you might want to check, to see how you feel about them now (this in itself might surprise you) and then to check again in two months to see how your attitude might have changed. It is a good idea to check your development every two or three months – download copies of this checklist so that you can keep a record of how you feel over time.

In this checklist:

1   = I find this difficult/I am uncomfortable with this.
2   = I can do this, but it takes quite a lot of effort.
3   = This is no problem to me.
4   = I positively enjoy this.

CHECKLIST 9

	1	2	3	4
Speaking up in a group situation.				
Organising my study material.				
Analysing new material.				
Grasping new concepts.				
Expressing my ideas verbally.				
Articulating my thoughts in my writing.				
Planning.				
Giving a formal presentation.				
Making notes from lectures.				
Making notes from reading.				
Taking control of my reading.				
Taking in information quickly under pressure.				
Standing up for my ideas.				
Working as part of a team.				
Explaining my course to others outside my study groups.				
Relating my study to other areas of life.				
Taking an overview of a task or situation.				
Working with academics/experts in my field.				
Facing new challenges.				
Meeting new people.				
Working outside my familiar field of knowledge.				
Being confident about what I know and think.				

© Lucinda Becker (2009), *The Mature Student's Handbook*,
Palgrave Macmillan Ltd

Your aim here is not to have each category reaching a '4' by the end of your course – this would be both unrealistic and, for most of us, undesirable. None of us want a complete personality change. It is more a case of **tracking change**, or recognising how you are developing and using this development to propel you forward. Propelling you forward might mean many things: a further course of study, a promotion at work, a whole new career.

Planning for change

Studying is addictive. Even if you have the firmest intention to take just one course, you can find that the lure of more studying creeps up on you. Of course, you might have times when it all seems to be too much, or when an aspect of your course disappoints you. You might also at times find yourself distracted from your studying, as the rest of your life encroaches, but as soon as the end is in sight you are likely to feel a sort of **pre-emptive nostalgia**. You begin to realise, almost imperceptibly at first, that you are going to miss studying. You will miss the challenge of taking in new material, the pleasure of sitting in a lecture hall and hearing a tutor giving you new information about your subject, the excitement of tackling new ideas and challenges. Most importantly, you will miss the new person you are becoming as a result of your studying: the person who feels more confident about a subject area and has the ability to stand up and talk about it confidently, the person who can escape for a few hours each day or week and give some time to reading, learning and reflecting on a subject area.

Although many students already have a framework mapped out for themselves, their course of study being part of an established pattern of life progression, they often still feel unaccountably depressed in the weeks and months after the completion of their course. Most realise that this is because their lifestyle has changed; few choose to analyse the details that make this move so deflating: the lack of challenge, the increase in life responsibility, the loss of study friendships. Mature students are often in a good position to avoid this loss, by taking on a further course of study – but making the perfect choice in this situation can be tricky.

If your addiction has taken you by surprise, you might be one of the large number of mature students each year who dash to take any course which will keep them studying. This can result in disappointment: a course that is not challenging enough, or one that appears to offer you a similar experience all over again, when in fact you would be happier moving on to a new area of challenge. You could end up in the wrong course, either in terms of subject area, ways of studying, or your overall career advancement.

Even if you have no intention at all of studying further in the future, you might want to heed the warning of thousands of other mature students and take this opportunity to plan what your ideal next course would be, just in case you decide to opt for some more studying. Checklists 10 and 11 cover some of the principal aspects of studying.

CHECKLIST 10

How I feel about my current course	I loved this	This was OK	I hated this
The topics I studied (list the six most prominent topics here and rank them):			
1.			
2.			
3.			
4.			
5.			
6.			
The style of studying:			
1. Lectures			
2. Seminars			
3. Class lessons			
4. Practicals and workshops			
5. One-to-one tutor sessions			
6. Dissertation/project supervisions			
7. Student-led sessions			
8. Placements			
9. Other:			

© Lucinda Becker (2009), *The Mature Student's Handbook*,
Palgrave Macmillan Ltd

C H E C K L I S T   1 0   (continued)

How I feel about my current course	I loved this	This was OK	I hated this
The ways of learning:			
1. Small group sessions			
2. Working in a team			
3. One-to-one sessions			
4. On my own			
5. Other:			
How I expressed my learning:			
1. Writing essays			
2. Speaking in seminars			
3. Producing a dissertation			
4. Giving presentations			
6. Producing case studies			
7. Writing reports			
8. Taking exams			
9. Speaking at conferences			
10. Applying my learning to my professional life			
11. Other:			

© Lucinda Becker (2009), *The Mature Student's Handbook*, Palgrave Macmillan Ltd

They ignore course titles and challenge you instead to think of the broader aspects of your studying life, so that you can match your requirements with the courses on offer to you.

These checklists are not exhaustive, but they will give you a good grounding in where you might move next. Once you have completed them you will be in the perfect position to ask for advice by:

-    Talking to your tutor. What options are available? How might they work in practice? What is involved? How does your tutor think you work best?
-    Discussing the situation with family and friends. They will have their own views on the impact your studying has had on your life (and on theirs), and how it might affect your situation in the future. You might be surprised by their views, and their opinions are likely to affect your decision.
-    If you are planning a professional development course, talking the matter through with your boss and colleagues will help. You might be tapping into a useful source of information about further courses, and there might be financial support available for you.
-    Checking on *all* courses open to you. Although it is always tempting to stay with your current institution, particularly if the practicalities of studying there suit you, it is still worth checking the internet and other sources to find out about a range of courses and what each has to offer.

Deciding on your next course of study – even deciding to undertake any more study at all – is a challenge, and taking this long-term view by planning early gives you the best possible chance of finding exactly the right course for both your current needs and your future development.

● Developing your career

In the same way that mature students are often taken by surprise by how much a course of study has changed them, and how keen they are to continue studying, they also tend to underplay the impact that studying is likely to have on their **career progression**. This leads them to undersell themselves in the job market. Even if they have no intention of changing their careers, they still sell themselves short by overlooking the progress they have made, and so not pushing for a promotion which would reflect their new level of knowledge and ability. They might also find that they no longer fit so easily into their original role within an organisation. Once you feel more confident, and become more used to speaking your mind and defending your position, it can be difficult to remain within your old pattern of working.

Over the years I have been able to compile a list of the top ten reasons mature students have given me as to why they do not intend to apply their newly acquired skills and knowledge to their career progression:

CHECKLIST 11

The practicalities of my next course	Definitely	Maybe	No
I would like to work in large groups			
I would like to do a placement			
I prefer exams to coursework			
I prefer coursework to exams			
I would like some one-to-one learning			
I want the chance to give presentations			
I would like to undertake a major project			
I want to move away from my current area of study			
A qualification matters to me			
I would like a higher-level qualification			
I would prefer learning with others face to face			
I would prefer distance learning			
I would like to be involved in e-learning via the internet			
I would like a flexible learning package			
I need to study part time			
I would prefer to study full time			
I might need an extended break in my study routine			
I need my course to be funded by my employer			
I would like a short course			
I am happy to study over 1–3 years			
I would like fully guided learning			
I am ready to undertake some independent research in my area			
I would like to travel as part of my course			
List in these free spaces any other factors you would like to take into account:			

© Lucinda Becker (2009), *The Mature Student's Handbook*, Palgrave Macmillan Ltd

1   I am retired, and just studying out of interest in this one area.
2   I am only doing this course because it relates specifically to my current job.
3   I am studying to take a break from my career because I was getting bored.
4   I cannot decide what to do in life, so a course seemed like a good idea.
5   Once I have taken this course I must get back to my 'real life'.
6   I have too much to do in life to sustain the energy required to do more than one course, or to apply it to the rest of my life.
7   My studying is just for me – it has nothing to do with the rest of my life.
8   I have deliberately chosen a non-vocational course out of interest, not because I expect it to change my life.
9   I need the money from my job, so I am not in a position to change career as a result of my course.
10   My course is not recognised by a professional body in my field, so it can have no relevance to my career progression.

If any of these statements ring true for you, it might be worth bearing in mind that none of them hold water for all of the students who have said them to me. I have helped retired students to take up freelance work as a result of their new level of expertise; I have seen students change direction altogether and enter new and successful careers; I have witnessed students who have 'leapfrogged' over colleagues to gain huge promotions on the back of courses which they undertook simply out of interest.

The point here is that you **cannot predict your future** – none of us can – and skills which you gain whilst studying, even if they are, at first glance, completely unrelated to your working life, can bring with them huge benefits for your career. There is nothing wrong, of course, with enjoying studying for its own sake and not deliberately relating your study life to your professional life as you study, but it makes sense to remain open-minded about where studying might lead you.

The management of your career might form part of your course – formal **career management modules** are compulsory for some courses; alternatively, you might choose to work with the Careers Service within your institution. It is certainly a wide area for consideration, and not one that can be covered fully here, but the checklists above will have given you ideas about how you have developed and what you have to offer your current employer, any future employer, or the world at large if you decide to work on a freelance basis.

The general approach to linking your study life to your career progression will involve a series of reflections on your development, and these may take place at any point in your course, either as part of a formal process or because you choose to consider the subject yourself. Broadly speaking, the process looks like this:

TAKE STOCK

- Use the checklists in this guide to evaluate how you have progressed, listing your key skills and finding examples to illustrate your skills and personal qualities to any potential employer.
- Keep checking your progress as your course develops - every two to three months is a good time to undertake this exercise.

ASSESS YOUR OPTIONS

- Talk to your fellow students, your tutor, and your family, friends and work colleagues to try to glean ideas about where you might go next in your career.
- As your plans develop, keep reporting back your progress to these key groups, so that you can get up-to-date advice and encouragement along the way.

DO YOUR RESEARCH

- Use your academic contacts to the full to find out about opportunities in your area.
- Enlist the support of your Careers Advisory Service as your plans progress.
- Research in professional journals and on the internet to make sure that you have considered all of the options.
- Remember that your fellow students are likely to have career experience and might be able to offer you useful 'inside information'.

TEST YOUR PLANS

As a career plan begins to emerge, test how realistic it is in two ways:

- By creating a career management action plan, and updating it periodically so that you keep up to date with your career needs.
- By writing a CV for yourself so that you can see, in black and white, just what a catch you would be.

Although you will find the exercises in this guide useful for the first three of these stages in the process, it is worth considering in more detail here the last stage: producing an ambitious but achievable career management action plan, and writing an effective CV.

● Career management action plan

An action plan gives you the chance to formalise what you intend to do to further your career whilst you are studying, helping you to make the best use of your time and opportunities, but also reducing your stress levels: once the plan is made, you will no longer have vague thoughts of your career planning hanging over you all of the time.

A career management action plan can be completed for whatever time scale suits you, from a few weeks to several years, depending on the length of your studying. You will not be able to complete it all in one session; instead, it will build up over time as new ideas come to you and new openings appear.

The action plan in Table 12 would work for a student who wishes to enter a career in Arts Administration. He has already worked in local theatres, but is now undertaking a year-long course in theatre management. Research has shown that, in the early stages of this career, the student might be required to work in Front of House (selling tickets, ushering, selling programmes etc.). Key skills required for entry into this career include excellent communication, teamwork, some knowledge of IT and as much experience in the theatre as possible.

Table 12 shows how his career management action plan would look by the end of his course; he would have been filling it out as he went along, giving himself the reassurance that he was making progress and helping to focus his efforts in the light of what he had achieved. Although some of these options will have been obvious to him at the outset, other ideas would only have come to him as his course progressed and he talked with his fellow students, his tutor and the Careers Service.

Table 13 is a blank template for you to complete. The timing column is left blank so that you can work to your own timescale.

● Curriculum vitae

An effective CV will be essential to your career progression, not just in presenting yourself to the world in the **best possible light**, but also to remind you of what you have to offer. Even if you do not intend to change career, a CV which reflects your newly acquired knowledge, experience and skills will be an inspiration to you, encouraging you to consider promotion within your existing career. A CV also works as a useful '**test document**': if you are thinking of changing career, producing a CV which is targeted for your newly chosen career area will allow you to see how well you would stand up amongst the competition. A CV is extremely difficult to produce by yourself: you will tend to be too modest, or to overlook key skill areas, or to downplay your achievements, so make sure that you get help when you come to write it.

Because your CV is an important **marketing tool**, it takes time and effort to think through all aspects of how it should best be created, and it takes research to work out how best to target it. However, it would be a good idea to make a CV for yourself right now, just to see what you might already be able to include, to remind yourself of what

When?	What?	How?	What next?
First term	1. Improve CV. 2. Front-of-house experience. 3. Presentation skills.	1. Visit Careers Service. 2. Volunteer with local drama society. 3. Help at departmental open days.	1. Completed. 2. Look for part-time work with local theatre. 3. Apply to help at International Students Welcome Week.
First vacation	1. Improve IT skills. 2. Earn some cash.	1. Drop-in sessions at IT skills base. 2. Contact events organisers.	1. Book for IT advanced evening class next term.
Second term	1. Improve presentation skills.	1. Give seminar presentations – join debating society.	1. Completed.
Second vacation	1. Theatre experience.	1. Vacation work for pantomime at a local theatre in publicity dept.	1. Apply for position at theatre, to start at the end of my course.
Third term	1. Assess Arts Administration career options.	1. Visit Careers Service; review options; update CV; offer to shadow professional?	1. Do as many placements as I can.

Table 12

you have to offer, and to identify areas where you might need to strengthen your skills base. You will need to keep your CV to two A4 sides long, and use the best-quality paper you can when you send it off. You may well end up with a 'master CV' which is much longer than this, from which you will draw for each job, depending on how you need to target the CV you send off.

There are many different layouts you might want to use, but the layout below gives you an idea of what works well for most mature students:

When?	What?	How?	What next?

Table 13

© Lucinda Becker (2009), *The Mature Student's Handbook*,
Palgrave Macmillan Ltd

Name
(The name you would like to be used at interview.)

Address
(On one line so that you don't waste space.)

Contact details
(Just a phone number and email address.)

Personal profile
(2–3 targeted sentences which describe you and highlight the skills, experience and personal qualities which will make you perfect for the job.)

Key skills
(Here list 4–6 key skills/experience areas for which the employer is asking, in a bullet-pointed list, and give an example for each skill which proves that you have that skill or experience.)

Education
(Here you will probably want to give your most recent qualification, with a little detail of how this relates to the job in question – earlier, less relevant qualifications can come later.)

Career history
(If your career to date links logically with the job for which you are applying, you will be able to list your most recent 3–4 jobs, with the duties you undertook and, crucially, the skills you acquired and the personal qualities you needed to be successful. Don't forget that employment here means any work you have done, which will include placements and voluntary work. You are trying to show that you can bring a positive benefit to the employer, so give examples where you can of how you improved things for your employers. If your previous jobs bear no obvious relevance to the prospective job, insert instead a 'functional' career history. This involves listing the general areas of work you have undertaken, without necessarily mentioning the names of employers. This allows you to present a long and complicated – and perhaps not obviously relevant – career history in the best possible light.)

Employment (or 'Early employment')
(If you have detailed your recent career above but have many years' experience before this, you can simply list here the jobs you have done, the employers and the dates. Take just one line per job, as this is a less enticing section than the one above. If you have created a functional career history above, list the employers here, but again with just one line per employer.)

Professional development
(This is where you include any training which will sell you to the employer. It need not be certified training; it might be an in-house course you once took, or on-the-job training you have received, as well as any professional development qualifications you have gained.)

Qualifications

(If you have itemised above your most recent qualifications, or if you have not mentioned education or qualifications at all yet, this is the place to list them. There is no need to waste space by listing them down the page – across the page will keep this section neat and ensure that you have enough space to sell yourself elsewhere.)

Additional information

(This is where you put information that is not necessarily a prime selling point but which you might like to include, for example your age, the fact that you are physically fit or that you are a car driver. You will also include aspects of your life which will positively sell you, such as a section for your hobbies and interests, especially if these help to show that you are the right sort of person for the job, along with any languages you speak, and/or the fact that you have a first aid or health and safety qualification.)

References available on request

(Probably you will not have space to list the full details of your referees here. The names of your referees are unlikely to sell you, and it is best to wait until an employer wants to contact them before you give the details; this gives you the chance to send your CV, application form and job description to your referees so that they know how to target their references.)

Beyond selling yourself in the most effective way, there are no rules about how a CV should be laid out, and you may well change the order of the entries above so as to highlight aspects of what you are selling. You are creating a **unique sales document**, and it will allow you to present yourself as you choose, thus giving you control over many aspects of the recruitment process. If you are interviewed based on your CV, you will know in advance the types of questions that might be asked, and this is a huge advantage at interview.

Nobody should ever have just one CV – it is a developing document, adapted for each new opportunity and always in the process of being updated as your skills and experience develop. Once you have produced your first CV in this layout, revisit it from time to time to see how much better you can make it – it is a challenge, but worth the effort; an impressive CV imbues you with confidence and courage for the career moves you want to make.

Last Thoughts

Embarking on a course of study as a mature student is not always an easy option – thank goodness. If it were easy, with few challenges and nothing to scare you, it would probably bore you to tears within a few weeks. You can expect to undergo an intellectual assault course, with new ideas being thrown at you, challenges to your preconceptions and, all the while, a constant demand for you to realign your way of thinking about your subject area and how you look at the world. How you look at yourself will change too – no more than you want it to, of course, but it will creep up on you, and you will start to revel in your new-found skills and begin to appreciate the process of learning.

The satisfaction of studying as a mature student will come and, as with most challenges in life, the exertion and anxiety will fade as the sense of achievement grows. Once you have mastered your subject area and, perhaps, gained a qualification, you will look back with pride on what you have achieved – and in the next moment you will be looking forward towards the next milestone on the journey. The journey is all your own, but I hope this guide will have made some of the travelling a little easier.

Index